The Stanza/*Ernst Häublein*

Methuen & Co Ltd

First published 1978
by Methuen & Co Ltd
11 New Fetter Lane London EC4P 4EE
© 1978 Ernst Häublein

Typeset by Preface Ltd
Salisbury, Wiltshire
Printed in Great Britain by
J. W. Arrowsmith Ltd., Bristol

ISBN 0 416 84600 9
ISBN 0 416 84610 6

Distributed in the USA by
HARPER & ROW PUBLISHERS INC
BARNES & NOBLE IMPORT DIVISION

To SUZY, MATHIAS and FRIEDRICH

Contents

1

Definitions of the stanza

The poetry of a people does not begin with the line but with
the stanza, not with metre but with music.
(Wilhelm Meyer, *Gesammelte Abhandlungen zur
mittellateinischen Rhythmik*, Berlin, 1905, I, p. 51,
my translation)

A group of lines of verse (usually not less than four),
arranged according to a definite scheme which regulates
the number of lines, the metre, and (in rhymed poetry) the
sequence of rhymes; normally forming a division of a song
or poem consisting of a series of such groups constructed
according to the same scheme. Also, any of the particular
types of structure according to which stanzas are framed.
(*Oxford English Dictionary*, def. 1)

This definition seems to cover the main familiar traits of the
stanza. Since it could be applied to forms of all periods, it provides an abstract ahistoric formula. If we compare the
stanzaic technique of various poets, we realize that stanzas
can be employed in many ways. Such differences reflect different concepts of poetic form. In examining what poets and
critics from the sixteenth century onwards have said about
the stanza, we shall discover stanzaic aspects typical of certain periods and shifting attitudes towards formal features of
poetry. Such a survey has never been undertaken before. It
may contribute to our understanding of poetry, because it
implies a brief history of poetic form.

Poets and early critics

One of the most famous statements on the stanza occurs in
George Puttenham's *The Arte of English Poesie* (1589),

which summarizes prosodical and poetic issues of Elizabethan poetry.

> Staffe in our vulgare Poesie I know not why it should be so called, vnlesse it be for that we vnderstand it for a bearer or supporter of a song or ballad, not vnlike the old weake bodie that is stayed vp by his staffe, and were not otherwise able to walke or to stand vpright. The Italian called it *Stanza*, as if we should say a resting place: and if we consider well the forme of this Poetical staffe, we shall finde it to be a certaine number of verses allowed to go altogether and ioyne without any intermission, and doe or should finish vp all the sentences of the same with a full period, vnlesse it be in some special cases, & there to stay till another staffe follow of like sort: and the shortest staffe conteineth not vnder foure verses, nor the longest aboue ten; if it passe that number it is rather a whole ditty then properly a staffe.
>
> (G. G. Smith (ed.), *Elizabethan Critical Essays*, II, p. 68)

Puttenham alludes to both the vernacular and the foreign traditions of stanzaic composition. He also distinguishes stanzaic poems by line length and equates syntactic and stanzaic unity. This tenet, which represents one of the main principles of Elizabethan verse, appears in a rather amusing form in George Gascoigne's *Certayne Notes of Instruction* (1575):

> In all these sortes of verses ... auoyde prolixitie and tediousnesse, and euer, as neare as you can, do finish the sentence and meaning at the end of euery staffe where you wright staues, ... for I see many writers which draw their sentences in length, and make an ende at latter Lammas: for, commonly, before they end, the Reader hath forgotten where he begon.
>
> (ibid. I, p. 56)

This demand for syntactic unity so typical of a prescriptive attitude pervades criticism and prosody until very recent times (Stewart, Kaluza).

Stanzas were not always highly favoured in the Renaissance. Poets adhering to principles of classical prosody like Campion tend to condemn the use of rhyme; others, like Daniel (1603), defend it. Most of them are less objective than Sir Philip Sidney, who, in his *Defence of Poesie* (1593), weighs the advantages of both modern accentual rhyming and quantitative rhymeless poetry. Although Ben Jonson wrote beautiful stanzas himself, he joined the battle. He composed a magnificently self-defeating, tongue-in-cheek invective entitled 'A Fit of Rhyme against Rhyme', complaining about the demise of perfect versing after 'the rack of finest wits' (rhyme) had been introduced. In his *Conversations with Drummond of Hawthorndon* (1618–19) he confesses that

> he had written a discourse of Poesie both against Campion & Daniel especially this last, wher he proves couplets to be the bravest sort of Verses, especially when they are broken, like Hexameters and that crosse Rimes and Stanzaes (becaus the purpose would lead him beyond 8 lines to conclude) were all forced.
>
> (Ben Jonson, *Works*, ed. C. H. Herford and Percy Simpson, I, p. 132)

Whereas Puttenham had explained the Italian derivation of stanza, others refer to the Greek etymology of *strophe*:

> Ein Satz oder Gesetze / (Στροφή,) ist ein gewisses theil eines Liedes/welches theil aus einer gewissen anzahl Verse/ die nachdem ihm der Tichter vorgenommen hat / in richtiger Länge/Art vnd Reimung zusammengesetzt sind/ bestehet/mit welchem die anderen Sätze alle/was Abmessung oder das *Metrum* anbelanget/genau übereinstimmen müssen . . .
>
> Woher bey vns der Satz/(man pfleget ihn bisweilen auch absonderlich einen Vers oder Versickel zu nennen)/seinen

Nahmen habe/ist leicht einzusehen/nehmlich/vom setzen/
weil die Verse darinn in gewisser Zahl und Abmessung
zusammengesetzet werden. Von den Grichen wird er
Strophe, das ist eine Wendung/genennet/weil man nach
Endung eines Satzes wieder vmbwendet / vnd nach der
ersten Abmessung von newem anfänget.

> (Johann Peter Titz, *Von der Kunst Hochdeutsche Verse*
> *und Lieder zu machen* (1642), M. Szyrocki (ed.), *Poetik*
> *des Barock* (Reinbek, 1968), p. 92)

A set (Στροφή,) is a certain part of a song that consists
of a certain number of lines composed of proper length,
kind of line, and rhymes, according to the poet's plan; with
this set all the other sets have to correspond exactly in di-
mension and metre . . .

It is easy to see where the German *Satz* (which, strangely
enough, is occasionally called verse or versicle, too) derives
its name: in fine, from 'to set', because verses of a certain
number and proportion are put together in it. It is termed
strophe by the Greeks, which means a turn, because after
completing one set, one turns around and begins anew, according to the first proportion.

> (my translation)

Johann Peter Titz continues the tradition of Opitz. He
defines poetry as 'made to be sung', a very familiar notion in
Elizabethan criticism and poetry. Like August Buchner
(1665), Albrecht Christian Rotth (1687) and many others
after him, Titz reiterates the demand for syntactic unity in
stanzas.

In 1702 Edward Bysshe contends that most stanzas contain
lines of different length and alludes to multi-stanzaic poems:

In the Poems compos'd of Stanzas, each Stanza contains a
certain number of Verses compos'd for the most part of a
different number of Syllables: And a Poem that is in

several Stanzas, we generally call an Ode; and that is Lyrick Poetry.

(*The Art of English Poetry*, p. 25)

The widespread predilection for classical odic forms in Augustan poetry, the impact of Cowley's experiments in the Pindaric vein and the ensuing vogue of Pindarics are reflected in Bysshe's reference to odes; they seem to be the epitome of lyric poetry. Bysshe also indicates what should be considered as stanzaic form:

The Stanzas employ'd in our Poetry cannot consist of less than three, and seldom of more than 12 Verses, except in Pindarick Odes.

(ibid. p. 26)

Dr Samuel Johnson's definition in his *Dictionary* (1755) was widely accepted and taken over verbatim by other eighteenth-century dictionaries, e.g. Sheridan (1780) and Walker (1791):

[*stanza*, Ital. *stance*, Fr.] A number of lines regularly adjusted to each other; so much of a poem as contains every variation of measure or relation of rhyme. Stanza is originally a room of a house, and came to signify a subdivision of a poem; a staff.

The Italian etymology (a room of a house) implies that stanzas are subordinate units within the more comprehensive unity of the whole poem.

Usually, Romantic poets do not refer to stanzas explicitly. However, both Wordsworth and Coleridge allude to them when discussing metre and rhyme in the *Lyrical Ballads*, which contain a good many poems written in stanzas.

There can be little doubt but that more pathetic situations and sentiments, that is, those which have a greater proportion of pain connected with them, may be endured in

metrical composition, especially in rhyme, than in prose.
The metre of the old ballads is very artless; yet they contain
many passages which would illustrate this opinion . . .

Now the music of harmonious metrical language, the
sense of difficulty overcome, and the blind association of
pleasure which has been previously received from works of
rhyme or metre of the same or similar construction, an
indistinct perception perpetually renewed of language
closely resembling that of real life, and yet, in the circum-
stance of metre, differing from it so widely – all these im-
perceptibly make up a complex feeling of delight, which is
of the most important use in tempering the painful feeling
always found intermingled with powerful descriptions of
the deeper passions.

> (*Preface to the Lyrical Ballads* (1802), D. J. Enright
> and E. de Chickera (eds), *English Critical Essays*, pp.
> 179–80)

For Wordsworth, the main function of metre, rhymes and–
by implication – stanzas consists in giving pleasure to the
reader and in mitigating the powerful effects of excitement
and passion transmitted by poetry. Wordsworth claims that
form prevents poetry from overwhelming the reader's – and
the poet's – emotions. Metrical form is characterized as 'superadded'.

This superficial, unorganic view, which implies a separa-
tion of form and content, is attacked in Coleridge's
Biographia Literaria (1815). Coleridge contends that prose
cannot simply be turned into poetry by engrafting metre
upon 'the language of real men', but that poetic form involves
poetic language; hence metre, rhyme and – by implication –
stanzas constitute poetry in conjunction with language.
Coleridge emphasizes the essential difference between poetry
and prose. Like Sidney and many others before him, he
stresses the mnemonic function of rhyme and stanzaic composition:

Would the mere superaddition of metre, with or without rhyme, entitle *these* to the name of poems? The answer is, that nothing can permanently please, which does not contain in itself the reason why it is so, and not otherwise. If metre be superadded, all other parts must be made consonant with it ...

... metre, especially *alliterative* verse (whether alliterative at the beginning of the words, as in 'Piers Plowman', or at the end as in rhymes) possessed an independent value as assisting the recollection, and consequently the preservation, of *any* series of truths or incidents.

(Enright and Chickera (eds), op. cit. pp. 194, 218)

Since stanzas, like other metrical phenomena, are elements of recurrence, Shelley may refer to them in the following passage from *A Defence of Poetry* (1821):

Hence the language of poets has ever affected a sort of uniform and harmonious recurrence of sound, without which it were not poetry, and which is scarcely less indispensable to the communication of its influence, than the words themselves ...

An observation of the regular mode of the recurrence of harmony in the language of poetical minds, together with its relation to music, produced metre, or a certain system of traditional forms of harmony and language.

(Enright and Chickera (eds), op. cit. p. 230)

Although their use is not mandatory, metric features contribute decisively to the musical effects of poetry. Thus, they enable the poet to sing his message of beauty and moral improvement, and to fulfil his function of prophet and legislator more effectively.

In his *Ästhetik* (1835) G. W. F. Hegel claims that stanzas are necessary structural markers, through which monotony can be avoided and distinct and variegated forms can be achieved. More important, he links stanzaic composition explicitly with the tone of lyric poetry:

> Unter den besonderen *Arten* der Dichtkunst ist es vornehmlich die *lyrische* Poesie, welche ihrer Innerlichkeit und subjektiven Ausdrucksweise wegen sich am liebsten des Reimes bedient und dadurch das Sprechen selbst schon zu einer Musik der Empfindung und melodischen Symmetrie, nicht des Zeitmasses und der rhythmischen Bewegung, sondern des Klanges macht, aus welchem das Innere sich selber vernehmlich entgegentönt. Deshalb bildet sich auch diese Art, den Reim zu gebrauchen, zu einer einfacheren oder mannigfaltigen Gliederung von *Strophen* aus, die sich jede für sich zu einem geschlossenen Ganzen abrunden.
>
> (*Ästhetik,* ed. F. Bassenge, II, p. 394)

> Among the specific *kinds* of poetry it is *lyric* poetry in particular which – because of its inwardness and subjective way of expression – favours the use of rhyme most strongly; consequently, it transforms the very act of speaking as such into a music of feeling and a melodious symmetry, not so much of measured time and rhythmical movement but of sound, out of which the inward soul resounds towards itself audibly. Therefore, this kind of rhyme use leads to more or less sophisticated structures of *stanzas*, each of which closes in a well-rounded unit.
>
> (my translation)

Hegel seems to characterize Romantic poetry in general, since he emphasizes the musical elements reflecting the harmony of the soul. He also differentiates lyric from epic poetry; the latter seems less suited for stanzaic composition:

> Die *epische* Poesie, wenn sie ihren Charakter mit lyrischen Elementen weniger untermischt, hält mehr ein in seinen

Verschlingungen gleichmässiges Weiterschreiten fest, ohne sich zu Strophen abzuschliessen.

(ibid. II, p. 394)

Epic poetry, if it is blended with lyrical elements to a lesser degree, tends to retain an intricate and yet regular mode of progression without stanzaic segmentation.

(my translation)

This tenet has been echoed in more recent evaluations of narrative stanzas (Rhyme Royal, *ottava rima*, Spenserian stanza).

Edgar Allan Poe stresses the principle of analogous repetition and contends that verse originates 'in the human enjoyment of equality, fitness'. Equality pertains to all elements of versification (rhythm, metre, etc.); it is also located in rhyme ('an equality in sound between the final syllables'), which leads to a discussion of the stanza:

> The consideration of this last equality would give birth immediately to the idea of *stanza* – that is to say, the insulation of lines into equal or obviously proportional masses. In its primitive, (which was also its best,) form, the stanza would most probably have had absolute unity. In other words, the removal of any of its lines would have rendered it imperfect. ... Modern stanza is excessively loose – and where so, ineffective, as a matter of course.
>
> ('The Rationale of Verse' (1843–8), J. A. Harrison (ed.), *The Complete Works of E. A. Poe*, XIV, p. 226)

Poe obviously dislikes the stanzaic tendencies in the poetry of some of his contemporaries. While it is true that many poets of the early nineteenth century disregard the concept of stanzaic unity so prevalent before 1800, Poe would certainly be appalled at the poetry of our own time. In the face of nineteenth-century attitudes towards poetic form, Poe's views appear to be remarkably conservative.

While Poe's stanzaic technique does not seem to be directly
indebted to 'primitive' models, Ezra Pound traces and revital-
izes a number of old forms, especially those of Provençal
poetry. Pound, who has influenced several generations of
both British and American poets, takes a historical stand. He
regards metrical technique as a necessary tool and demands
that poets should master 'all forms and systems of metric'
('Credo', 1918). This includes stanzas as well:

> Symmetry or strophic forms naturally HAPPENED in lyric
> poetry when a man was singing a long poem to a short
> melody which he had to use over and over. There is no
> particular voodoo or sacrosanctity about symmetry. It is
> one of many devices, expedient sometimes, advantageous
> sometimes for certain effects.
>
> ('Treatise on Meter' (1934), D. M. Allen and W. Tallman
> (eds), *The Poetics of the New American Poetry*, p. 63)

Symmetry cannot serve for every subject; but this does not
entitle the poet to neglect form completely.

Pound's friend and pupil T. S. Eliot also asserts that
stanzas have to accord with the poet's intention, who may, or
may not, choose stanzaic forms:

> ... any form may be more appropriate to some periods
> than to others. At one stage the stanza is a right and natural
> formalization of speech into pattern. But the stanza – and
> the more elaborate it is, the more rules to be observed in its
> proper execution, the more surely this happens – tends to
> become fixed to the idiom of the moment of its perfection.
> It quickly loses contact with the changing colloquial
> speech, being possessed by the mental outlook of a past
> generation; it becomes discredited when employed solely
> by those writers who, having no impulse to form within
> them, have recourse to pouring their liquid sentiment into
> a ready-made mould in which they vainly hope that it will

set. ... Elaborate forms return: but there have to be
periods in which they are laid aside.

('The Music of Poetry', *Partisan Review*, IX (1942), pp.
463–4)

The notion that stanzas may be historically 'dated' has been
repeated by many contemporary poets. Louis Zukofsky, who
quotes Pound's statement on the musical origin of stanzas
almost verbatim, claims that 'existence does not foster this
technique at all times indiscriminately' ('A Statement for
Poetry' (1950), Allen–Tallman (eds), op. cit. p. 146). It is
very interesting that Zukofsky holds that stanzas should
incorporate several subordinate units of meaning: 'The least
unit of a poem must support the stanza; it should never be in-
flicted on the least unit' (ibid. p. 146).

Robert Lowell regards the stanza as a whole to be 'rounded
out' by a climax. He confesses:

I seesaw back and forth between something highly metrical
and something highly free; there isn't any one way to write.
But it seems to me we've gotten into a sort of Alexandrian
age. Poets of my generation and particularly younger poets
have gotten terribly proficient at these forms. They write a
very musical, difficult poem with tremendous skill,
perhaps there's never been such skill. Yet the writing seems
divorced from culture somehow.

('Interview with Frederick Seidel' (1963), G. Perkins
(ed.), *American Poetic Theory*, p. 320)

As late as 1971 Ted Hughes also conceives of metrical
devices as one among many possibilities of poetic form:

I use them here and there. I think it's true that formal patterning of the actual movement of verse somehow includes
a mathematical and a musically deeper world than free
verse can easily hope to enter. It's a mystery why it should
be so. But it only works of course if the language is totally

alive and pure and if the writer has a perfectly sure grasp of
his real feeling . . . and the very sound of metre calls up the
ghosts of the past and it is difficult to sing one's own tune
against that choir. It is easier to speak a language that
raises no ghosts.

('Ted Hughes and Crow. An Interview with Egbert
Faas', *London Magazine*, New Series, X, no. 10
(January 1971), p. 20)

While Hughes reluctantly admits the function of strict
forms, the poets associated with Robert Creeley and Charles
Olson are determined to lay the ghosts of the past and reject
stanzas and other features of symmetry. In Olson's view, they
are not suitable for the composition of what he calls
'projective', i.e. open, verse. Since poetry arises from a 'composition by field' involving an 'energy discharge' from the
poet, Olson concludes with Creeley that 'FORM IS NEVER
MORE THAN AN EXTENSION OF CONTENT'. Consequently, fixed
forms have to be abandoned. Form emanates from the
energy of the field; it grows out of strings of perception and a
processual ('kinetic') way of writing. Structure depends on
syllables and lines formed by breathing units. Projective
verse, therefore, involves a 'breaking away from traditional
lines and stanzas', which stand for inherited, non-projective
poetry ('Projective Verse' (1950), Allen–Tallman (eds), op.
cit. pp. 147–58).

Allen Ginsberg also develops 'breath units', which he calls
'variable stanzaic units' ('*Notes for Howl and Other Poems*'
(1959), Allen–Tallman (eds), op. cit. pp. 319–20); these are
actually long lines which serve as a method of notation.
Ginsberg's 'When the Mode of the Music Changes the Walls
of the City Shake' (1961) conveniently summarizes the attitude of many poets of our time:

Trouble with conventional form (fixed line count & stanza
forms) is, it's too symmetrical, geometrical, numbered and

pre-fixed – unlike to my own mind which has no beginning
and end, nor fixed measure of thought (or speech – or
writing) other than its own cornerless mystery ... always
bearing in mind, that one must verge on the unknown,
write toward the truth hitherto unrecognizable of one's
own sincerity, including the unavoidable beauty of doom,
shame and embarrassment, that very area of self-recogni-
tion ... which formal conventions, internalized, keep us
from discovering in ourselves and others ... the mind must
be trained, i.e. let loose, freed – to deal with itself as it
actually is, and not impose on itself, or its poetic artifacts,
an arbitrarily preconceived pattern (formal or Subject) ...
(Allen–Tallman (eds), op. cit. pp. 324–5)

Ginsberg would object if we labelled this kind of poetry form-
less; as for Olson, making is discovery for Ginsberg, and since
'Mind is shapely, art is shapely' (Allen–Tallman (eds), op.
cit. p. 326).

We have seen that many modern poets do not subscribe to
such tenets, nor do all of Olson's and Creeley's followers
adopt these views. From the writings of Denise Levertov, for
example, there emerges a new concept of stanzaic structure:

It usually happens that within the whole, that is between the
point of crystallization that marks the beginning or onset
of a poem and the point at which the intensity of contem-
plation has ceased, there are distinct units of awareness;
and it is – for me anyway – these that indicate the duration
of stanzas. Sometimes these units are of such equal duration that one gets a whole poem of, say three-line stanzas, a
regularity of pattern that looks like, but is not, pre-
determined.
('Some Notes on Organic Form' (1965), Allen–Tallman
(eds), op. cit. pp. 314–15)

Levertov, who seems indebted to Aristotle, the neo-Aristotelians, Coleridge and Creeley as well, tries to avoid the tyranny of fixed forms; this does not mean. however, that stanzas must be regarded as superfluous and detrimental to poetry. Although for her 'Form is never more than a revelation of content', and although poetry is not tied to identical stanzaic recurrence, stanzas retain a few important functions within the poetic whole:

> Rhyme, chime, echo, repetition: they not only serve to knit the elements of an experience but often are the very means, the sole means, by which the density of texture and the returning or circling of perception can be transmuted into language, apperceived.
>
> (Allen–Tallman (eds), op. cit. p. 314)

Whereas Olson, Creeley and Ginsberg initiated the revolt against rhyme, stanza, order and symmetry, Levertov presents a viable theory of form, which combines both traditional and modern views.

We have thus surveyed a variety of concepts of stanzaic composition, ranging from the emphasis on fixed patterns, clear divisions and subdivisions, order and symmetry, to the discovery of intrinsic form revealing its peculiar shape through its content, from closed to open forms.

Modern prosodists

Since it has been the main concern of modern prosody to investigate aspects of rhythm and stress, the stanza has been generally treated with benign neglect. The approach of describing and classifying, familiar since Puttenham and Gascoigne, has been systematized during the last 100 years. J. Schipper (1881-8), G. Saintsbury (1906–10), M. Kaluza (1909) and Enid Hamer (1930) have written pioneer works, on which later metrists have heavily – sometimes too heavily – relied. The procedure is relatively simple: stanza forms are characterized and traced historically, with general statements on the practice of individual poets. After Schipper and Saintsbury, it has been the main task to bring examples up to date and to condense the predecessor's efforts. In more recent years, notably in Germany (Touber, 1968; Schlawe, 1972), metrists have enlisted the help of computers to compile lists of stanza forms of various poets and periods. Since classifications cannot go beyond features of extrinsic form, aspects of meaning are usually ignored or discussed at random.

Historical metrists like F. B. Gummere (1901), W. Meyer (1905), Gay Wilson Allen (1935) or Frank M. Tierney (1971, 1973) have dealt with the stanza or particular forms in a less positivistic manner. Period studies have yielded important results concerning certain stanzas (J. E. Bernard, Jr, 1939; K.-U. Prasuhn, 1974). One of the most impressive – and least speculative – attempts of this kind is Friedrich Gennrich's *Grundriss einer Formenlehre des mittelalterlichen Liedes* (1932): he argues that medieval metrical structures originated from musical structures. He criticizes descriptive metrics, because it overemphasizes the rhyme scheme. Gennrich contends that stanzas do not depend on the rhyme scheme but represent rhythmical and melodic wholes based on musical structures.

The followers of Sidney Lanier's (1880) 'musical' theory, among them R. M. Alden (1903), T. Omond (1903), M. W. Croll (1923, 1929), E. Smith (1923), G. R. Stewart, Jr (1925, 1930) and D. A. Stauffer (1946), view the stanza as 'a group of the line groups' (Lanier, *The Science of English Verse*, 3rd ed. (Baltimore, 1945), p. 239) or 'units of tertiary rhythm in poetry, unitary groups of verses combined to a uniform and more or less symmetrical pattern, the structural arrangement being usually marked by rime' (E. Smith, *The Principles of English Metre* (London, 1923), p. 194). In a way Henry Lanz also belongs to this school, since he defines the stanza ' as a specific system of melodic tensions and relaxations caused by some specific arrangement of the vowel-keys' as represented by rhymes, which are recurrent 'harmonic groups' (*The Physical Basis of Rime* (Palo Alto, 1931), p. 154). Although its musical premisses have been severely attacked in recent years, notably by linguists, the musical theory contributed considerably to our understanding of time structure and musicality in verse. It did not, however, advance stanzaic problems beyond conventional classification.

The acoustic school of W. Sievers (1901), F. Saran (1906) and E. W. Scripture (1929), although it managed to refute some misconceptions about pitch, loudness, timbre and time, was too preoccupied with measuring verse by means of the oscillograph to devote much labour to the stanza.

Similarly, linguistic metrists are usually content with the descriptive approach to stanzas. Most of them deal with more basic aspects of metrical analysis. Consequently, followers of linguistic structuralism have bypassed the stanza completely, because 'higher-order metrical constructs' (J. Lotz, 'Metric Typology', in T. A. Sebeok (ed.), *Style in Language* (New York, 1960), p. 147) or 'larger metrical phenomena, like line structure or stanza pattern, have been satisfactorily described and classified in the past' (S. Chatman, *A Theory of Meter*, p. 10). Stanzas are considered as 'effective "packages" of metrical units' to be grouped with 'auxiliary matters' (J. Malof, *A Manual of English Meters*, pp. vi–vii). The most recent vogue of generative metrics (Halle–Keyser, 1971; J. C. Beaver, 1971; J. Ihwe, 1972; and G. F. Wedge, 1972) is exclusively preoccupied with stress analysis.

All these approaches are basically descriptive, some of them even prescriptive and dogmatic. Except for occasional hints, the problem of meaning as related to stanzaic form has been generally overlooked or even avoided, mainly because it seems to defy objective analysis. Furthermore, metrists are uncommonly conscious of the confines and boundaries of their discipline: problems of meaning are considered to belong to the domain of semantics and poetics. Strangely enough, students of poetic form, e.g. P. Fussell (1965) or H. Gross (1964), delegate the problems of stanza structure back to prosody; in other words, we are again offered classifications and descriptions, together with allusions to technical features of individual poets, which are frequently unreliable because of the excessive – and occasionally justified – distrust of statistical evidence.

Since stanzas are subordinate units within the larger whole of the poem, two main approaches seem to be called for: the investigation of stanzaic unity, on the one hand, and a discussion of the relationship between the parts (stanzas) and the whole of the poem, on the other. Although these aspects are implied in some studies, e.g. those of Barbara H. Smith, Elder Olson and the present writer, we shall have to break some new ground in these areas. After a descriptive chapter, we shall deal with various devices by which poets have achieved stanzaic unity; Chapter 4 centres on the relations between stanzas and the structural implications of stanzaic composition.

2

Stanza forms

> But to treat of all the different Stanzas that are employ'd, or
> may be admitted in our Poetry, would be a labour no less
> tedious than useless, it being easie to demonstrate that they
> may be vary'd almost to an Infinitie.
>
> (Edward Bysshe, *The Art of English Poetry* (1702), p. 26)

Stanza forms are determined by the rhythmic mode, the
number of lines and feet per line, and the pattern of end or
terminal rhymes. For reasons of space, we shall disregard
unrhymed stanzas. We differentiate rising (iambic and
dactylic) and falling (trochaic and anapaestic) metres. Since
English verse is predominantly iambic, the simplest way to
chart stanza forms is to indicate the rhyme scheme and the
number of feet, e.g. $a_4b_3a_4b_3$ for the ballad stanza, $ababcc_5$ for
the *Venus and Adonis* stanza. Sometimes it is advisable to
count syllables in order to mark *catalexis* (omission of the
last syllable(s) in falling metres) or *hypercatalexis* (addition
of slack syllables in rising metres, especially in disyllabic and
trisyllabic rhymes). This is particularly important when
normal lines alternate with catalectic or hypercatalectic ones,
a frequent feature of stanzas with varying line length (non-iso-
metrical or heterometrical stanzas). Various positions of end
rhymes account for the rhyme schemes: rhyme repetition
(e.g. aa); alternate (interlocking, crossed) rhymes (e.g. abab);
intermittent rhymes (e.g. abcb); and envelope (inserted)
rhymes (e.g. abba).

When we attend only to the rhyme scheme of stanzas we
notice that they are made up of smaller units, that is the
primary unit of a stanza form consists of subdivisions or
basic units. These units are composed of variously grouped

lines. We can repeat a rhyme once or twice and arrive at the basic units aa and aaa; we can also introduce a second or third non-identical rhyme and arrive at the basic units ab and abc. Thus lines can be connected by repetition and alternation. We can combine rhymes according to these two principles and arrive at the basic units aba, aab and abb. Most familiar stanza forms consist of these seven basic units, i.e. immediate constituents. They can be arranged into stanzas by repetition and alternation. Since these two principles of arrangement are employed in the construction of both immediate constituents and stanza forms, we can call them generative principles. As in *Formal Linguistics*, these abstract formulae can be used to generate all possible forms, even those that have never entered the mainstream of the poets' inventory. It is difficult to explain why certain forms have been chosen while many others have been neglected or rejected by poets. If, as W. Meyer contends (see above, p. 1), stanza forms originated from musical structures, we might look for a clue in the patterns of melodies: there are hardly any melodic units whose subdivisions consist of more than two phrases, which ideally correspond to lines. The most frequent forms reflect conventional melodic structures; rarely used or rejected stanzas may not be based on musical prototypes.

The following generative procedures provide a descriptive framework which we shall have to concretize; the less important forms are given in parentheses.

1 Immediate constituents are repeated identically at least once, e.g. abab, ababab, abcabc (aaaa, abaaba, aabaab, abbabb).

2 Immediate constituents that are generated by the same structural principle (repetition or alternation) are connected, e.g. aabb, aabbcc, aabbccdd, abba, aabccb (abca, abbcbb, abccba, etc.).

3 Immediate constituents that are generated by different

    structural principles are connected, e.g. aaba, abcdd, ababb, aabab (abaa, abcc, etc.).

4 Immediate constituents are repeated identically and connected with constituents of the same structural principle, e.g. ababcdcd, ababbcbc, ababcdcdefef (abcabcdef, etc.).

5 Immediate constituents are repeated and connected with constituents of another structural principle, e.g. ababcc, ababbcc, ababccc, ababbcc, ababccb, ababbcbcc, abcabcdd, etc.

In what follows we shall survey and define the most familiar stanza forms of English verse. We shall proceed descriptively according to the number of lines and refer to well-known examples. Space does not permit us to expatiate on the handling of particular forms by different poets. The most profitable way would be to compare the syntax, the rhythm, the stanzaic segmentation, the rhyme technique and the tone of poems composed in the same stanza, and to remember the implications of genre in evaluating stanzaic technique. We shall also have to bear in mind that stanza forms as such are merely moulds and containers, vessels to be filled, which may support but will never constitute meaning in poetry. It is therefore impossible that elements of meaning inhere in stanza forms. If this observation is not heeded, forms 'take on a strange phantom-life of their own, independent of the poem in which they occur' (*TLS* review of R. S. Crane's *The Languages of Criticism* (1954), p. 572). Prosodists disqualify themselves when they characterize a stanza form as 'remarkably naif and infantine', 'a stately and leisurely metre', 'a brisk and businesslike metre with a martial suggestion', etc. (Hamer, *The Metres of English Poetry*, pp. 176, 181, 165), or when they ascribe to a stanza form 'dignified movement' (L. J. Zillman, *The Art and Craft of Poetry* (New York, 1966), p. 73) or 'a certain degree of passion and seriousness' (Fussell, *Poetic Meter and Poetic Form*, pp. 147–8). Usually such generalizations are based on the treatment of a given stanza by a particular poet, or even on a particular poem. Although Goethe alludes to 'great mysterious effects' inhering in different poetic forms (*Gespräche mit Eckermann*, 25 February 1824), and although Gascoigne notes (Smith (ed.), op. cit. I, p. 56) that certain stanzas evince some affinity with specific topics and literary kinds (amatory verse, complaints, hymns, narrative verse), 'there is nothing in the nature of these kinds that makes a given stanza obligatory' (Fussell, op. cit. p. 134).

Couplets

Couplets of four (tetrameter, short couplets) or five feet (pentameter, heroic couplets) are employed most frequently. Except in epigrams, couplets rarely appear as stanzas, although we should mention Frank O'Hara's trimeter couplets in 'Poem' and Thom Gunn's pentameters in 'Moly'. Usually couplets are parts of a longer poem. Some metrists, therefore, do not regard them as stanzas proper. Since the precursor of the syllabic-accentual tetrameter was the Old English four-stress couplet, it is the oldest form of metrical verse in English poetry. The paraphrase of the *Paternoster* (twelfth century), *The Owl and the Nightingale* (thirteenth century) Chaucer's *Booke of the Duchesse* and Gower's *Confessio Amantis* represent the most prominent examples before 1500. Concerning its later use, we should compare Jonson's 'Come, my Celia, let us prove', Milton's *L'Allegro* and *Il Penseroso*, Marvell's 'To His Coy Mistress', Butler's *Hudibras*, Sir Walter Scott's *The Lay of the Last Minstrel*, Byron's *The Bride of Abydos*, and Keats's 'To Fancy', 'To the Poets' and 'On the Mermaid Tavern'. In the popular verse of the fifteenth and sixteenth centuries we find short couplets with a varying number of slacks between stresses, e.g. in Skelton and pre-Shakespearian drama.

The heroic couplet is the more important of the two. It was

introduced into English poetry by Chaucer in *The Canterbury Tales* and *The Legend of Good Women*, and employed by Lydgate (*The Siege of Thebes*), Spenser (*Mother Hubbard's Tale*) and Marlowe (*Hero and Leander*). Its development is linked to the rise and perfection of blank verse in the sixteenth century, which, as John Thompson has shown, represents an extension of the tetrameter line. The name heroic couplet derives from the vogue of heroic drama culminating in Dryden, who commended Waller's and Denham's handling of couplets in lyric poetry. At the same time there was a marked tendency to explore the possibilities of the closed (end-stopped) couplet, notably in the poetry of Pope; he constructed magnificently antithetical, witty and succinct epigrammatic units, which were to inspire Byron in *English Bards and Scotch Reviewers*. The use of the heroic couplet decreased after its heyday in the eighteenth century, although Roy Campbell and Robert Frost handle it with considerable skill.

The hexameter couplet, which dominated French and German drama in the seventeenth century, has never been popular in English. Alexandrines are occasionally used in closural lines, as in the Spenserian stanza, or coupled with heptameters, with which they form the Poulter's Measure (see 'Quatrains', below).

Tercets

Tercets, like couplets, appear more frequently as parts of bigger units than as stanzas. The *terza rima*, an iambic pentameter tercet developed by Dante, is composed of alternate rhymes (aba bcb cdc, etc., yzyz). It can hardly claim the status of a stanza because of the uninterrupted linkage of its consecutive units. It was taken over by Chaucer (*Complaint to His Lady*) and employed by Wyatt (*Penitential Psalms*), Sidney (in twelve poems of his *Old*

Arcadia and in *Psalme 7*), Byron (*The Prophecy of Dante*) and Shelley (*Prince Athanase, The Triumph of Life*), who also constructed a *terza rima* sonnet in *Ode to the West Wind* (aba bcb cdc ded ee), Auden (*The Sea and the Mirror*), MacLeish ('Conquistador'), Empson and Thom Gunn ('The Annihilation of Nothing').

The triplet aaa, on the other hand, displays certain features of formal unity. It occurs surprisingly often in the seventeenth century, both as tetrameter and pentameter, e.g. in Herbert's 'Paradise' and 'Trinity Sunday', in Herrick's 'Whenas in silks my Julia goes' and Lovelace's 'I cannot tell who loves the skeleton'. Browning seems to favour it, as do Thomas Hardy and John Masefield.

Quatrains

The quatrain is the most common stanza form in European and American poetry. There are five variants of it: several versions of ballad metre, the heroic stanza (abab$_5$), the envelope or *In Memoriam* stanza (abba$_4$), the aabb stanza and the Rubaiyat stanza (aaba$_5$). The ballad metres represent divisions of longer couplets with alternate or intermittent rhymes: abcb$_4$ or abab$_4$ (Long Metre = LM), a$_4$b$_3$c$_4$b$_3$ or a$_4$b$_3$a$_4$b$_3$ (Common Metre = CM), abcb$_3$ or abab$_3$ (Half Metre = HM) and ab$_3$c$_4$b$_3$ or ab$_3$a$_4$b$_3$ (Poulter's Measure or Short Metre = PM or SM). The original couplet lines contain eight (LM), seven (CM) or six (HM) feet each; the Poulter's Measure, whose name derives from the poultryman's practice of selling a dozen eggs and adding two eggs to the second, connects a hexameter and a septenar line. Like Anglo-Saxon alliterative verse, these folk metres may vary the number of slacks between stresses. The caesura, which is always fixed, reflects the original structure of the long lines. Scansion follows the rules of stress verse in that the lines are basically dipodic, i.e. primary stresses in the first and third feet alternate with secondary ones in the second and fourth feet. If there is no fourth foot, we read a pause, which indi-cates that CM, HM and SM originated from LM. We can test this theory, which has been proposed by Stewart and Malof, by reading hymns, nursery rhymes and ballads aloud. Melodies and settings confirm this view. Ballad metres are extremely widespread in English poetry. They are probably the only consistently used forms, even in modern poetry, which has seen a 'ballad revival' (A. B. Friedman, 1966): abab forms outnumber by far all the other stanzas in twentieth-century poetry; they figure prominently in the poetry of Hardy, Ransom, Hope, Gunn and Hill.

The heroic stanza ($abab_5$) probably has its roots in LM quatrains. The first example occurs in Wyatt's 'Heaven and earth, and all that hear me plain'. In the sixteenth century it shared the popularity of all pentameter lines. Dryden used it in *Heroic Stanzas on the Death of Oliver Cromwell* and in *Annus Mirabilis*. It is sometimes called Hammond's metre because James Hammond employed it in his *Love Elegies* (1743). Thomas Gray made it famous in his *Elegy Written in a Country Churchyard* (1750), from which it derives its name of elegiac stanza. However, the elegiac tradition after Gray failed to adopt the form, which has always been moderately popular.

The *In Memoriam* stanza gained its reputation through Tennyson, although he did not invent the form. Ben Jonson had already used it in 'If Beauty be the Mark of Praise'. It hardly reappears after Wilde's 'The Sphinx'. Like most quatrains, it splits easily in the middle, although it is more closed than isometric aabb stanzas.

The Omar Khayyam quatrain or Rubaiyat stanza ($aaba_5$) was adapted to English use by FitzGerald in his translation from the Persian original. Frost employed it in 'Desert Places' and modified it slightly in 'Stopping by Woods'.

Stanzas composed of two or more couplets tend to disintegrate into their components except in heterometrical stanzas such as the so-called Horatian ode. Marvell's 'An Horatian Ode Upon Cromwell's Return from Ireland' has a tetrameter and a trimeter couplet (aa_4bb_3); Collins's 'Ode to Evening' consists of unrhymed pentameter and trimeter couplets. Renaissance and seventeenth-century poets were fond of the isometric iambic version $aabb_4$, which they preferred for love lyrics, e.g. Marlowe's 'Come live with me and be my love', Ralegh's 'Reply' and Donne's parody 'The Baite'; C. Day Lewis continues the tradition of this poem in 'Come live with me and be my love' ('Two Songs'). The stanza is fairly frequent in English poetry, also in a trochaic version.

Cinquains

Five-line stanzas or cinquains are much less common than quatrains. Only the ababb and abaab stanzas, which may be extensions of LM and CM, have been used at all frequently, e.g. in Sidney's *Astrophil and Stella*, 'Song ix', *Psalme* 4, Donne's 'Hymn to God, my God', Herbert's 'Aaron' (ababb), 'The World', 'The Glimpse' and Robert Graves's 'Ulysses' (abaab).

Sixains

Six-line stanzas or sixains have always abounded in English poetry. The most popular form has been the stanza which Shakespeare used in *Venus and Adonis* and which was highly recommended by Puttenham ($ababcc_5$). Many poets after 1500 favoured it because of its closural couplets. Neither the tetrameter nor the pentameter form was confined to sixteenth-century poetry (Sidney, Watson, the *Miscellanies*). The stanza was used for solemn themes as well as for shorter amorous and extended narrative poems. Its tripartite structure, which also constitutes the end of the Shakespeare sonnet, consists of two identical elements (abab, two *Stollen* as *Aufgesang*) and a conclusion (cc, *Abgesang*) and thus compares to canzone, Minnesinger and Meistersinger structures. Günther Müller locates the same pattern in the Italian sonnet, which is thus related to the ababcc stanza ('Die Grundformen der deutschen Lyrik' (1941), in E. Müller (ed.), *Morphologische Poetik* (Darmstadt, 1968), p. 142). Many three-stanza poems written in this metre resemble the sonnet. Two such poems by Watson contained in *England's Helicon* (nos 26 and 58 in Rollins's edition) were transformed into sonnets by A. Nixon and A. Craig. Occasionally eighteen-line poems read like structural imitations of the stanza they are written in: two parallel or analogous stanzas are concluded by a third which departs from the structural analogy, e.g. Sidney's *Lady of May* 3, *Old Arcadia* 36, 37, 46, and *Certain Sonnets* 19 (Ringler's edition). If we compare the poems by Sidney and Shakespeare with Donne's 'The Expiration', Dryden's 'Song to a Fair Lady', Cowper's 'The Castaway', Wordsworth's *Laodamia* and 'I wandered lonely as a cloud', Shelley's 'Hymn to Apollo', Arnold's 'To Marguerite', John Wain's 'Time was', Theodore Roethke's 'Four for Sir John Davies' and Thom Gunn's 'Mirror for Poets', we can judge how differently this magnificent form has been handled in English verse.

Like the aabab and abaab stanzas, the tail-rhyme stanza aabccb (or aabaab) could be an extension of ballad metres, especially in its heterometrical shape of $aa_4b_3cc_4b_3$. It originated in medieval Latin *versus caudati* and French *rime couée*. English tail-rhyme stanzas first appeared in the thirteenth century and were employed in lyrics and romances, hence the name Romance Six. Chaucer parodied these in *The Tail of Sir Thopas*, from which it derives its third name. The stanza, which figures prominently in sixteenth-century drama and in religious and secular verse up to Herbert, was used in various shapes by Gray ('Elegy on a Favourite Cat'), Smart ('Song to David'), Wordsworth ('Three years she

grew'), Browning ('Rabbi Ben Ezra'), Bridges ('Nightingales')
and Hardy ('The Sigh'), among others. There is an eight-line
version $aaa_4b_3ccc_4b_3$, which is familiar from *Noah's Flood* in
the Chester Cycle, and a ten-line form, which appears as late
as in Swinburne's 'A Child's Laughter' ($aaaa_4b_3cccc_4b_3$).

The Burns stanza $aaa_4b_2a_4b_2$ ('To a Louse', Wordsworth's
'At the Grave of Burns') may go back to Provençal models of
the eleventh century. It is also found in medieval English
romances and miracle plays.

In modern poetry, the traditional six-line stanzas (including the ever-present aabbcc and ababab forms) have been
generally neglected. But we find a few less familiar forms:
Thom Gunn, like Yeats, Joyce, Berryman, Dylan Thomas
and Richard Wilbur before him, seems to prefer the abcabc
stanza ('Lofty in the Palais de Danse'), which Herbert,
Browning and Swinburne employed a few times ('Church-
Monuments', 'Among the Rocks', 'Itylus', 'The Oblation').

Seven-line stanzas

In *Troilus and Criseyde* Chaucer created a seven-line stanza
composed of a pentameter rhyming ababbcc, the Chaucer or
Troilus stanza. After his brilliant handling of it in *The
Parlement of Fowles* and some of the *Canterbury Tales*, it
became the main stanza of the Chaucerians: Lydgate, Occleve, Hawes and Barclay in England, and Henryson,
Dunbar and King James I of Scotland. The latter's *Kingis
Quair* may explain the name Rhyme Royal, but the term may
derive from the French *chant royal* as well. The *Troilus*
stanza remained extremely popular until Wyatt and the
Mirror for Magistrates. It was recommended for serious
verse, historical narratives and political poems by Gascoigne
and Puttenham. It was noted for its amplitude and flexibility,
and for the closural implications of its couplet, which gives
firm contour to the stanza. When the syntax delineates the tripartite structure ab–ab–bcc, the first two sections are called

pedes and the conclusion a *cauda*. After Spenser's *Fowre Hymnes* and Shakespeare's *The Rape of Lucrece*, the stanza appeared with a closing alexandrine in Milton's 'On the Death of a Fair Infant' and 'The Passion'. This form was employed by Chatterton in his *Balade of Charitie* and by Wordsworth in 'Resolution and Independence'. The *Troilus* stanza proper was revived by William Morris in *The Earthly Paradise*; Morris usually abides by 5 : 2 or 4 : 3 divisions, or fills the stanza with one syntactic unit. John Masefield is not the only modern poet to remember the form ('Dauber', 'The Widow in Bye Street'): Graves handles it very skilfully in 'Rocky Acres'; it also appears in Auden's 'The Shield of Achilles' and in Anthony Thwaite's 'Death of a Rat'. In modern verse, however, the stanza is not nearly as popular as ballad metres.

There is no other seven-line stanza that can rival the *Troilus* stanza. Donne seems to have invented the pentameter ababccc stanza, possibly an isometrical version of Surrey's $a_4b_3a_4b_3cc_4c_5$ ('O happy dames'). Donne uses it with a closing alexandrine in 'The Good-morrow' and a final tetrameter in 'Loves Deitie'. Wordsworth's 'The Afflictions of Margaret' has tetrameters throughout; Shelley varies the line length in 'Mutability' $(a_3b_2a_3b_2cc_3c_2)$. One of the few modern poets who chose the stanza is Theodore Roethke, who employed it in 'I Knew a Woman'. Since the last line of each stanza contains a closural parenthesis, Roethke obviously takes the form as an extension of the *Venus and Adonis* stanza rather than as a variant of Rhyme Royal. The poem reads like an imitation in the metaphysical vein. There are several experimental stanzas with different rhyme schemes, the most prominent being the $ababccb_5$ of James Thomson's *City of Dreadful Night*, where the cc lines usually have feminine rhymes.

Eight-line stanzas

Eight-line or octave stanzas are very common in English

poetry. Some of them are double quatrains, like the ababcdcd stanza or the brace octave abbacddc. Both forms demand the poet's skill, if he wants to avoid splitting. Usually the unity of such stanzas is very precarious. In many cases the rationale for choosing an eight-line instead of a four-line stanza is hard to see. Drayton solves the problem of stanzaic integrity by anaphoras in 'I pray thee leave, love me no more' ($a_4b_3a_4b_3c_4d_3c_4d_3$ with feminine b and d rhymes). Herbert, as usual, marks formal closure with short lines in 'Humilitie'; Wordsworth links the halves syntactically and logically in 'To a Lady' ($ababcdc_4d_3$). The brace octave, which occurs less frequently than the double ballad, may also be found in modern poets. It appealed to Yeats, Edward Thomas, W. Owen, Philip Larkin and Robert Conquest ('A Problem', a truly excellent example).

The ryhmes of the ababccdd stanza seem to suggest sufficient closure. This stanza was occasionally employed in the sixteenth and seventeenth centuries, e.g. in Gascoigne's 'The Lullaby of a Lover' and Beaumont's (or Fletcher's?) 'Lovers rejoice' (from *Cupids Revenge*), both of which clearly accentuate the stanzaic openings. Wordsworth selected it for 'The Solitary Reaper' ($aba_4b_3ccdd_4$) and his 'Ode to Duty', whose stanzas close in impressive hexameter lines.

This form is much rarer than the *ottava rima* ($ababab cc_5$), one of the most important stanza forms in English poetry. This stanza, which may go back to the ballade (ababbcbc) or the Sicilian *strambotto*, was perfected by Boccaccio, Ariosto, Tasso and Camões. It was usually preferred in epic poetry. Wolfgang Kayser stresses its two-part shape, which suggests a division after the alternate rhymes and a contrast, summary or epigrammatic conclusion in the couplet (*Kleine deutsche Versschule* (Berne, 1971), p. 47). Schiller tried to characterize the *ottava rima* in the following elegiac distich:

Stanze, dich schuf die Liebe, die zärtlich schmachtende
– dreimal

Fliehst du schamhaft und kehrst dreimal verlangend zurück.
(Werke in drei Bänden, ed. H. G. Göpfert (Munich, 1966), II, p. 726)

Ottava rima, created by tenderly languishing love,
Thrice you bashfully flee, thrice you return with desire.

(my translation)

Wyatt introduced it into English and proved that it is well suited for lyrics. Surprisingly, many of his fifteen-odd poems in this metre consist of only one stanza. Spenser chose the form for *Virgil's Gnat* and *Muiopotmos*; Sidney composed two stanzas each in *Old Arcadia* 35 and 54, both of which exhibit strictly end-stopped lines and closural emphasis in the couplets; he also used it in *Other Poems* 4, a long epyllion. After Harington's and Fairfax's translations of Ariosto and Tasso, Daniel's *Civil Wars* and Drayton's *Barrons Wars*, it obviously fell into oblivion, although Milton took it for the coda in Lycidas, where it symbolizes the speaker's consolation. Byron reclaimed it in *Beppo, The Vision of Judgment* and *Don Juan*.

In Byron's hands, the stanza turns into an extremely pliable instrument of wit. He uses unusual, outrageously unorthodox rhymes, which provide the frame for his pyrotechnics. Sometimes he seems to consider the stanza merely as a formal shell, which he fills very freely and without excessive regard for its divisions. His stanzas, which are rarely linked through enjambement, generally remain units of meaning within which narrative and descriptive passages mingle with the narrator's digressions and parentheses, his jibes and ironic meanderings, which occasionally make 'the stanza stammer', as he puts it in *The Vision of Judgment* (stanza 57).

Keats's *Isabella, or the Pot of Basil* demonstrates how differently the *ottava rima* can be constructed. Keats demarcates the divisions much more faithfully that Byron or Shelley (*The Witch of Atlas*); he very often emphasizes the couplet closurally. Yeats is the only modern poet who made extensive use of the stanza. It occurs in major poems like 'Among School-Children', 'Coole Park and Ballylee, 1931', some parts of 'Vacillation', in 'The Gyres', 'The Circus Animals' Desertion' and in two stanzas of 'Sailing to Byzantium'.

Nine-line stanzas

Since the Spenserian stanza evolved out of the ballade, we should mention this Provençal form ($ababbcbc_5$). It occurs predominantly in stanzaic poems composed of three stanzas plus a four-line *envoi*. It was the favourite form of François Villon. Chaucer used it in *The Monkes Tale*; some nineteenth-century poets, like Dobson, Henley and Swinburne, obviously inspired by Théodore de Banville, joined in the revival of the ballade proper. Spenser experimented with the stanza in the November Eclogue of his *Shepheardes Calender*. By adding an alexandrine to the ballade, he extended it into a nine-line stanza, the so-called Spenserian stanza ($ababbcbc_5c_6$), in the *Faerie Queene*. That the structure of linked rhymes appealed to Spenser is also borne out by the pattern of the Spenserian sonnet.

Usually Spenser does not divide the stanza into more than two or three sections; he prefers subdivisions of 5 : 4 and 6 : 3 lines. The most impressive stanzas are those in which the syntax spans all the lines and throws full emphasis on the alexandrine. Although the form lends itself to couplet closure, Spenser likes to isolate the last line, which frequently rounds off the stanza and functions as closure, a feature typical of Renaissance poetry. The alexandrine contains summaries, maxims and comments by the narrator, but also marks off different stages of the narrative. Since most of the pentameters exhibit between three and four stresses, the rhythm is generally smooth and fluid. Spenser likes to proceed in a leisurely way by employing Elizabethan catalogues and strict line divisions. Considering that the stanza was invented for an epic poem, it is surprising that we do not encounter many run-on lines. Furthermore, the syntactic divisions are rarely placed within the lines. Spenser avoids stanzaic enjambement and feminine rhymes, although the latter increase slightly in Books IV to VI.

After Thomson (*The Castle of Indolence*), Shenstone ('The School-Mistress') and Beattie ('The Minstrel'), the Spenserian stanza appears in Byron's *Childe Harold's Pilgrimage*. Byron finds the stanza 'difficult, because it is like a sonnet, and the finishing line must be good' (*Medwin's Conversation of Lord Byron* (1824), ed. E. J. Lovell, Jr (Princeton, 1966), p. 236). He likes to segment the stanza into exceedingly many small subdivisions (usually more than four) in the first two books. This indicates that he may be indebted to the couplet style of Beattie (Prasuhn); in the earlier books, the rhymes barely unify the great number of syntactic subdivisions within the stanza. In Books III and IV the number of stanzas with autonomous sections decreases. The rhythm is usually harsher in the early books, smooth and dynamic in the later ones. Rhythmic urgency increases through run-on lines, internal caesuras and stanzaic enjambement. Byron stresses stanzaic openings and de-emphasizes closure, a very frequent feature of Romantic poetry. He obviously regards the stanza as a skeleton that can be filled freely and flexibly, and which therefore disintegrates occasionally under the strain of his impulsive and enthusiastic tone.

While Byron accommodates the Spenserian stanza to a great variety of moods, Shelley, who used it in 'Dedication of *The Revolt of Islam*. To Mary —', in 'Stanzas Written in Dejection' and in *Adonais*, limits it to reflective and elegiac contexts. Consequently the syntax of *Adonais* is usually contained, its rhythm less varied and urgent than in Byron. Shelley also endows the first line with strong emphasis; occasionally the last two lines are treated as closural couplets.

Keats adopted the stanza at the beginning ('Imitations of Spenser'), in the middle (*The Eve of St Agnes*) and towards the end (*The Cap and Bells*) of his poetical career. In *The Eve of St Agnes*, we find traces of Byron's technique, e.g. initial emphasis, faulty rhymes and numerous subdivisions. Like Spenser, Keats stresses the alexandrine's closure and thus provides the stanzas with firm contours. Nevertheless, his stanzas are not comprehensive units, nor do they exhibit smooth and fluid rhythms. If it were not for the difference in tone and genre and the sensuous richness of sounds, Keats's Spenserian stanzas would resemble those of Byron. Evaluations of stanzaic technique ultimately depend on aspects of genre and period features. After Keats, Tennyson ('The Lotos-Eaters', ll.1–45) was one of the few poets to choose this stanza. In view of the fact that poets tend to avoid excessively long stanzas, the Spenserian stanza has had a remarkable history.

Stanzas of ten, eleven or twelve lines hardly occur in English poetry, although some individual forms have become famous, especially those employed by Keats: 'Ode to a Nightingale' has a heterometrical ababcdecde stanza which looks like a truncated Italian sonnet; in 'Ode on Melancholy' and 'Ode on a Grecian Urn' Keats uses a very similar isometrical ten-liner with occasional modifications in the sestet. In 'Ode to Autumn' we find an eleven-liner constructed on the same principles. Shelley has a twelve-line stanza in 'Hymn to Intellectual Beauty'. Most of these longer stanzas, from Elizabethan madrigal stanzas to Shelley's 'Autumn: A Dirge', Arnold's 'Thyrsis' and Swinburne's 'Ave atque Vale', are in some way heterometrical.

Classical stanza forms

We should include a few forms that were developed in classical languages. Some of them were adopted by English poets during the Renaissance, when the *Areopagus* of Sidney, Spenser and Harvey experimented with quantitative metres.

The sapphic stanza

English poets knew the sapphic four-liner from Catullus and Horace. It was first employed by the Greek rhapsode Sappho of Lesbos (*fl. c.* 600 BC). It consists of three hendecasyllabic (eleven syllables) sapphics (–⏑–⏓–⏑⏑–⏑–⏓) and an Adoneus (–⏑⏑–⏓). The classical habit of stanzaic enjambement was often imitated by English poets. Sidney used the stanza in 'If mine eyes can speake to doo harty errande' (*Old Arcadia* 12); he employs rhymes (abab) in 'O my thoughtes' sweete foode, my onely owner' (*Certain Sonnets* 5). This poem shows that Sidney went beyond the controversy about rhymes, because it combines quantitative and rhyming-accentual principles. In his *Defence of Poesie* (1593), Sidney attributes 'musick', 'sweetnesse' and 'majestie' to both. Campion was less conciliatory on these matters in *Observations in the Art of English Poesie* (1602), where he discusses a few unorthodox sapphics of his own; his 'Come let us sound with melody the praises', a paraphrase of Psalm 19, is a fine poem, whose quantities are faithfully delineated by the music. Isaac Watts dimly imitates the original metre in 'The Day of Judgment'; this poem, which is basically accentual, provided the model for a great number of English sapphics from Southey to Swinburne and Pound ('Apparuit'). In a way, all four-line stanzas with a short final line may be indebted to the sapphic stanza.

The alcaic quatrain

The alcaic quatrain, named after Alkaios of Mytilene (*fl. c.*

600 BC), consists of two eleven-syllable, one ten- and one nine-syllable alcaic lines; the stanza is less important in English, although Clough, Swinburne and Tennyson ('Milton') used it. It may have influenced the Horatian quatrain aabb discussed above (see 'Quatrains').

The Pindaric ode

The Pindaric ode is a fixed form composed of a triad of stanzas: the *strophe* (turn) and *antistrophe* (counterturn) follow the same pattern; the *epode* (stand) departs from it. The number of triads contained in a poem is not limited. In Pindar's *Odes*, which were written for choric presentation and dances in public celebrations (443 BC), the stanzas are long heterometrical units. English examples of this form are very rare: Ben Jonson's 'To the immortall memorie, and friendship of that noble paire, Sir Lucius Cary and Sir H. Morison' and Gray's 'The Bard' are well-known examples. Cowley's *Pindaric Odes* (1656) do not imitate the structure but try to capture the exalted and powerful tone of Pindar. Cowley initiated a vogue of heterometrical and hetero-stanzaic poems, which attracted Dryden ('Alexander's Feast') and Tennyson ('Ode on the Death of the Duke of Wellington'). Pindarics were regarded as fit vehicles for revelling in the newly discovered Longinian sublime.

Formal ambiguity

We have already noted that in some stanza forms the rhyme scheme fails to demarcate clear and convincing subdivisions: the rhymes of the *Venus and Adonis* stanza suggest three obvious smaller units, which poets conscious of the stanzaic skeleton tend to imitate syntactically; other stanzas of more than four lines, notably isometrical ones, imply several possibilities of differentiating their parts. Thus the cinquain ababb suggests either two alternate rhymes and one concluding line

or a tercet plus couplet. The Rhyme Royal can be divided
into a quatrain plus bcc or a cinquain of potential subordinate units plus a couplet. The Spenserian stanza implies
two basic divisions: the syntax can accentuate the two
quatrains and isolate the alexandrine, or the first quatrain
can be separated from the tercet bcb to be followed by the
couplet cc. Many more examples could be adduced. If we are
aware of formal ambiguity, we are in a better position to
gauge the structuring of stanzas. Some poets observe only
one structural implication rigidly but impressively; others
may betray a limited concept of form. Poets utilizing a
variety of inherent patterns (or none at all) may want to
escape structural monotony. Thus ambiguous forms can be a
yardstick for stanzaic technique, because they show how
much the poet reflects upon the stanza as form. They may
also reveal the stylistic features of different poems, poets and
periods, because they help us to register technical
characteristics much more subtly than the crude distinction
of poets who did, and those who did not, adhere to the
structural implications of clearly delineated stanzas.

Heterometrical stanzas

In heterometrical stanzas the subdivisions are emphasized by
line length. Thus line length contributes to a more definite
stanzaic expectation in the reader. Formal ambiguity can be
reduced by longer and shorter lines. The pattern of stanzas
based on strings of couplets, batches of alternate rhymes and
monorhyme stanzas, which are all basically open and suggest
continuation, receive rhythmically unifying contours. Since
differences in line length figure most prominently in the
poetry of Herbert, we shall select a few examples from *The
Temple*. We shall indicate syllables rather than feet in the
following stanza forms.

As in Common Metre poems, the rhyme scheme of

Herbert's 'Divinitie' is supported by line length: $a_{10}b_8a_{10}b_8$. Since we quickly realize it to be a concomitant norm of all the *parts* of this stanza, line length does not function as a structuring device of stanzaic *unity*. The same holds for the $a_8b_4a_8b_4$ stanza in 'The Search', or the $a_4b_{10}a_4b_{10}$ stanza of 'The Posie', which could easily be continued, and for most tail-rhyme stanzas. We may discover the same regularity in the $a_7a_3b_7c_7c_3b_7$ pattern of 'The Invitation' and 'The Banquet', through which single identical parts are delineated, but which does not constitute a stanzaic expectation.

If, however, the line length implies a *stanzaic* norm, it contributes to formal unification. If we read 'Divinitie' and 'The Method' ($a_4b_8a_8b_4$) aloud, we notice the difference: while each stanza of the former consists of two identical parts, the latter is one unit whose rhythmic implications compare with the rhymes of the *In Memoriam* stanza. The effect depends on what Albert McHarg Hayes (1938) calls counterpoint: 'no lines which rime together have also the same number of syllables' ('Counterpoint in Herbert', p. 52). Rhythmic identity can also be attained by 'off-balance stanzas', in which there is one shorter or longer line, as in 'Vertue' (aba_8b_4), and by irregular or symmetrical stanzas, as in 'Aaron' ($a_6b_8a_{10}b_8b_6$) or 'Easter-Wings' ($a_{10}b_8a_6b_4a_2c_2d_4c_6d_8c_{10}$). These poems also show that formal unity through rhyme pattern or line length are two different principles, which can, of course, cooperate. Many heterometrical poems by Herbert demonstrate that short lines tend to coalesce with adjacent ones through enjambement. Occasionally this indicates that many short lines originated from splitting long lines. We shall discuss further aspects of short and long lines in Chapter 3.

Stanzaic poems

There are a few fixed forms consisting of one or several stanzas. We call such forms stanzaic poems. Most of them have been imported into English poetry. Some of them, like haiku and the ghazal, have never been developed beyond the stage of experimentation. Most of the longer forms have been incorporated into the tradition of English poetry. The following survey proceeds from small to large forms.

Haiku

This Japanese poem comprises exactly seventeen syllables which are distributed in lines of five, seven and five. It can be traced back to the sixteenth century. It flourished in Japan until the nineteenth century. Originally haiku dealt with a season or New Year month, mainly employing natural images and symbols. It became very popular in France around 1920. Most of the English imitations are adaptations of the technique: some imagists constructed shorter poems with natural subjects and imagery, e.g. Pound and Amy Lowell; Frost, Aiken, Yeats and Auden, among others, were possibly influenced by the haiku vogue. In recent years (1968), Richard Wright ('Four Haiku') and Etheridge Knight reclaimed the original form; I quote an example from Knight's 'Haiku':

> The falling snow flakes
> Can not blunt the heart aches nor
> Match the steel stillness.

> ('Haiku', no. 6, *The Norton Anthology of Modern Poetry*, p. 1305)

The tanka, a Japanese poem of five lines with a total of thirty-one syllables (5, 7, 5, 7, 7), is considerably older but less important for English than haiku.

Ghazal

The ghazal (or ghasel, 'web') is an Eastern form which dates back to the eighth century. It was familiarized by Goethe (*West-östlicher Divan*), Schlegel, Rückert, von Platen and

Weinheber in Germany. It consists of five to fifteen couplets; the rhyme of the first couplet is repeated in all even lines, the odd lines are rhymeless. The ghazal is mentioned here because this curious form was obviously introduced into English poetry by Jim Harrison (*Outlyer and Ghazals,* 1969–71). His long and rhymeless couplets – usually six of them – are disjointed sequences whose 'only continuity is made by a metaphorical jump' (Harrison); see no. XXI ('He sings from the bottom of a well').

Triolet

The triolet is the smallest stanzaic poem derived from the French. Its shape depends on two recurring identical lines, which are capitalized in the following scheme: ABaAabAB. This eight-line form, which originated in the thirteenth century, is the simplest version of the rondel. After its nonce appearance in the religious poetry of Patrick Carey (1651), the triolet was taken over by English poets in the wake of Daudet's and Théodore de Banville's attempts to revive old forms. Dobson ('Rose-Leaves'), Henley ('Easy is the triolet') and Bridges ('When first we met', 'All women born are so perverse') used this intricate and demanding form with ease and good effect. Barbara Howes's three triolets in 'Early Supper' (1956) show that it appeals to modern poets as well.

Villanelle

The villanelle ('rustic song') usually consists of five aba tercets and a concluding abaa quatrain. The first and third lines recur according to the pattern A_1bA_2 abA_1 abA_2 abA_1 abA_2 abA_1A_2. The form is based on an Italian folksong of the late fifteenth century; it flourished from the time of the Pléiade until the beginning of the seventeenth century. Like many other French forms it was popularized in English by the group of poets associated with Dobson and Henley. It is, however, one of the few forms that has been adopted by several twentieth-century poets: after Wilde's 'Theocritus' it appeared in E. A. Robinson's 'House on a Hill' and Pound's 'Villanelle: The Psychological Hour'. Empson used it in 'Villanelle' and 'Missing Dates', Auden in 'My Dear One is Mine' (*The Sea and the Mirror*) and 'Time will say nothing but I told you so'. It occurs as late as 1952 in Dylan Thomas's 'Do not go gentle into that good night', a truly excellent poem.

Rondel

The rondel proper comprises thirteen or fourteen lines with the rhyme scheme ABbaabABbabbaA(B). There are a few earlier forms of it, among them a ten-line form Abb abA abbA, which Chaucer inserted at the end of *The Parlement of Fowles*, ll. 680–9. This type shows the influence of Deschamps. Chaucer's *Merciles Beaute*, with three recurrent lines (AB_1B_2 $abAB_1$ $abbAB_1B_2$), was imitated by Occleve. Lydgate's 'These sevyn virgyns' has fourteen lines. Dobson wrote this form in 'Too hard it is to sing'. There are several examples by Henley, Gosse and Stevenson.

Rondeau

The rondeau derives from shorter forms like the triolet and from the rondel, with which it is occasionally confused. It consists of stanzas of five, three and five lines constructed on two rhymes (aabba aab aabba). Since the beginning of the first line, usually a tag of no more than four syllables, is repeated as *rentrement* (R) after the eighth and last line, the rondeau has the structure aabba aabR aabbaR. It is one of the most consistently used forms in French poetry, and one of the most significant stanzaic poems in English. Wyatt composed about nine rondeaus, e.g. 'What vaileth trouth?', 'For to love her', 'Helpe me to seke'. He liked the *rentrement* so much that he attached it to a variety of stanzas in other poems. Except for occasional experiments by Charles Cotton

('Thou fool, if madness be so rife', etc.) and some examples in *The Rolliad* (1784), the rondeau did not really flourish before the end of the nineteenth century. Again, Dobson ('You bid me try', 'With slower pen', 'In after days', 'When Burbage played') and Henley ('When you are old', 'What is to come') favour the form. Dobson wrote about twenty-eight, Henley fourteen, Gosse eleven and Lang five rondeaus. After Dowson, Stevenson, Bridges, Untermeyer and Brander Matthews had tried their hands at it, John McCrae ('In Flanders' Field'), Auden ('The Hidden Law') and Barbara Howes ('Death of a Vermont Farm Woman') wrote rondeaus.

Swinburne constructed an eleven-line version (abaR bab abaR) from it, which he called 'rondel' or 'roundel'. Since the poems contained in *A Century of Roundels* all have a *rentrement*, they should not be regarded as rondels but as short rondeaus.

Sestina

The sestina is the last – and most fascinating – stanzaic poem to be discussed here. It consists of six stanzas of six lines each, which are followed by an *envoi* of three lines. The end words of each line are taken up in the next stanza according to a fixed numerical order, usually 6-1-5-2-4-3 (*retrogradatio cruciata*), until they are repeated in their original sequence in the *envoi*. This is the arrangement in the sestinas of its originator, the troubadour Arnaut Daniel. The form is actually a very sophisticated version of correlative verse (Fucilla, 'A Rhetorical Pattern', p. 30, n. 6); it may be more fitly called a unified 'pattern of stanzas' than a 'single-stanza poem' (Shapiro and Beum, *A Prosody Handbook*, p. 120). The sestina has always excited the minds of theorists and practitioners alike. It represents a European phenomenon (János Riesz) which has attracted a great number of poets up to our own time: the troubadours after Daniel; Dante and Petrarch, and their innumerable imitators; Michelangelo, Sannazaro, d'Annunzio, Ungaretti; the Spaniards Montemayor, Herrera, Lope de Vega, Cervantes; the Portuguese Lois de Camões; the French poets Pontus de Tyard, de Grammont; the Germans Weckherlin, Opitz, von Abschatz, Gryphius, von Zesen, Eichendorff and Borchardt.

The first English sestina was composed by Spenser. In the August Eclogue of his *Shepheardes Calender* (1579) he uses the arrangement 6-1-2-3-4-5 developed by de Cetina, which, although less complex, is by no means easier than 6-1-5-2-4-3. For the first time in the sestina's history, Spenser connects the stanzas by enjambement. Sidney inserted three sestinas in his *Arcadia*; one of them ('Ye Goteheard Gods') is a double sestina consisting of twice six stanzas and a three-line *envoi*, which can already be found in Dante and Petrarch. 'Farewell, ô Sunn' exhibits the rhyme scheme of the *Venus and Adonis* stanza (ababcc$_5$), which Sidney knew from Pierre de Loyer's *Erotopegnie* (1576), and which was also adopted in one of the two examples by Drummond of Hawthorndon. Rhyming sestinas were first constructed by Pontus de Tyard (abcbca). This technique generates several different stanzas within the sestina.

English sestinas reappear in the nineteenth century. Of the numerous examples quoted by G. White in *Ballades, Rondeaus, Chants Royal, Sestinas, Villanelles*, etc. (1887) and elsewhere we should note Swinburne's 'Love shut up with wings' and Kipling's 'Sestina of the Tramp-Royal'. Pound returned to troubadour models in 'Sestina: Altaforte', an impressive dramatic monologue that influenced Donald Hall's sestina 'Hang it all, Ezra Pound, there is only the one sestina'. Auden wrote several sestinas, e.g. 'Making, Knowing and Judging' (his Oxford inaugural address), 'Having a Good Time' and 'Paysage Moralisé', which recalls Sidney and Spenser. In 'Kairos and Logos' Auden composed a sequence of four sestinas, which follow the arrangement 3-1-5-2-6-4. In the second chapter of *The Sea and the*

Mirror, Sebastian sings a sestina which alternates a 3-6-4-1-2-5 and a 2-4-6-5-3-1 rhyme order. Roy Fuller, George Barker, Donald Justice, David Lougée and W. S. Merwin have tried the form. A more recent example is Diane Wakoski's 'Sestina from the Home Gardener' (1968), a valediction poem with difficult end words and extremely fluid syntax.

The thirty-six lines at the beginning of Section II in Eliot's 'Dry Salvages', although reminiscent of some of the sestina effects, should not be grouped with it, because they lack the principle of revolving end words according to a numerical pattern.

Sestinas have been used for amorous, pastoral, reflective-philosophical, meditative, didactic and political subjects. They appear as single poems as well as in epic and dramatic contexts. The sestina is one of the most exacting and rewarding – and controversial – forms, which has challenged the technical potential and the supreme sense of artifice in the best poets.

3
Stanzaic unity

The middle . . . is the least interesting, the beginning the next
most interesting, and the end the most interesting.
(Paul Fussell, Jr, *Poetic Meter and Poetic Form*,
p. 179)

Several definitions of the stanza quoted in our first chapter
imply the notion of stanzaic unity. It is, therefore,
remarkable that there has never been a systematic attempt to
demonstrate how it may be achieved. Obviously the stanza's
integrity as a whole should be investigated before we
approach the relationship of particular stanzas within the
poem. In order to set stanzas off against each other, the
opening or the concluding section or both may be emphasized. Usually poets intent on stanzaic unity prefer stanzaic
closure to stanzaic opening, because features implying
stability, resolution, release of tension, equilibrium, co-
herence, completion, finality and fulfilment of expectation
seem to convey a stronger sense of integrity than openings,
although there are historical differences. Several of the following closural devices derive from Barbara H. Smith's
Poetic Closure. Unfortunately, Smith deals only with the
problem of how *poems* end and fails to explore the stanzaic
ramifications of her approach.

Any part constituting a subordinate whole may display
initial as well as closural characteristics, even though these
may turn out to be more relative than those discovered in
poetic wholes: 'My lute awake!' and 'Now cease, my lute!'
(Wyatt) highlight the beginning and the end of the poem very
conspicuously. Stanzaic openings, on the other hand, mark
the stages of poetic development within a poem; stanzaic conclusions within a poem do not necessarily imply cessation. In

order to avoid confusion between poetic and stanzaic opening and closure the following examples are as a rule taken from stanzas within the poem.

We also have to bear in mind that stanzaic unity depends either on features within a given stanza or on those in adjacent stanzas. Any kind of stanzaic repetition, e.g. stanzaically repeated structures, stanzaic anaphoras, and other correspondences, and most types of refrain, etc., constitute stanzaic wholes which the reader can recognize as such only *ex posteriori*: we tentatively gauge the integrity of each stanza of Carew's 'Ask me no more' retrospectively after the second stanza, whereupon we expect the recurrence of the structural stanzaic principle, i.e. we perform what Smith terms 'retrospective patterning'. In what follows we shall try to list various means by which stanzaic unity can be effected. We shall notice that several devices contributing to stanzaic unity are frequently combined. We shall not aim at an exhaustive catalogue of such devices. The reader should become aware of the problem and discover such features on his own.

Stanzaic opening

Any unusual and striking beginning may arrest our aural and visual attention and thus demarcate stanzaic wholes. In 'The Prohibition' Donne employs an initial line of six syllables which is rhythmically set off from the ensuing ten-syllable lines. Its integrative force increases palpably because the stanza contains no corresponding short lines. Donne does, however, repeat the phrase 'Take heed of loving mee' in line 8, which neatly closes the stanza with a sort of internal refrain that recurs in each stanza:

> Take heed of hating mee, ...   (l. 9)
> If thou hate mee, take heed of hating mee.   (l. 16)

The device is even more striking if the initial line is extremely short, as in Herrick's 'An Ode for Him' ('Ah, Ben'), Stanley's

'The Exequies' ('Draw near') or Elizabeth Bishop's 'The Man-Moth' ('Here, above').

An exceedingly long line functions quite similarly:

> RING out your belles, let mourning shewes be spread,
>   For love is dead:
>
> Weepe, neighbours, weepe, do you not heare it said,
>   That Love is dead?
>
> Let Dirge be sung, and Trentals rightly read,
>   For Love is dead:
>
> Alas, I lie: rage hath this errour bred,
>   Love is not dead.
>   (Sidney, *Certain Sonnets* 30, ll. 1-2,
>   11-12, 21-2, 31-2)

Sidney obviously lengthened the initial line deliberately in order to achieve the stanzaic opening: the first four syllables of each stanza could be connected immediately with the second line; the remainder of each first line complements but does not constitute the connection.

The rhythmic impact of such stanzaic openings increases, if certain words or phrases are repeated in the first line:

> O Death, O Death, rock me asleep,
>
> My pains, my pains, who can express?
>
> Alone, alone in prison strong ...
>
> Farewell, Farewell, my pleasures past!
>   (Rochford (?), 'O Death, O Death', ll. 1,
>   10, 19, 28)

The *ploce* in ll. 1 and 10 and the *epizeuxis* in ll. 19 and 28 contribute to a passionate tone and may thus be grouped with devices of emotional heightening such as exclamations, interjections and expletives:

My lute, alas! doth not offend,
>   (Wyatt, 'Blame not my lute', l. 8)

Alas, alas, who's injur'd by my love?
>   (Donne, 'The Canonization', l. 10)

O how feeble is mans power,
>   (Donne, 'Song. Sweetest love, I do not
>   goe', l. 17)

O no, O no, tryall onely shewse . . .
>   (Sidney, *Certain Sonnets* 24, l. 10)

Loe where she comes along with portly pace,

Behold whiles she before the altar stands,

Ah when will this long weary day have end,
>   (Spenser, 'Epithalamion', ll. 148,   223,
>   278)

This device of initial emphasis depends very much on the tone and the intention of the poem. Such tags are likely to appear in exalted, passionate and rhapsodic contexts. They are favoured by poets employing predominantly personal and emotional speakers (Donne, Herbert, Crashaw, many Romantic and Victorian poets). They seem especially apt for odes and elegies, where they are by no means confined to *poetic* openings. If we include the use of *apostrophe*, we may discover a marked predilection for stanzaic openings and a lack of emphasis on closure in the nineteenth century. This view, which could be substantiated quantitatively, seems warranted in the light of the fact that many Romantics and post-Romantics are less bent on distinct stanzaic contours. The reader may test this tenet by comparing the frequency of initial and closural interjections, exclamations and expletives in Romantic poems, e.g. Byron's *Don Juan*, 'Canto I'. While most modern poets, if they use stanzas at all, seem hardly con-

cerned about stanzaic boundaries, nineteenth-century poets
at least retained clear and rhythmically impressive openings:

> Thrice welcome, darling of the Spring!
> > (Wordsworth, 'The Cuckoo', 'O Blithe
> > New-comer!', l. 13)

> Ye blessed Creatures, I have heard the call . . .

> Behold the child among the new-born blisses,

> O joy! that in our embers . . .

> Then sing, ye Birds, sing, sing a joyous song!

> And O, ye Fountains, Meadows, Hills, and Groves,
> > (Wordsworth, 'Ode. Intimations of
> > Immortality', ll. 36, 85, 133, 172, 191)

Initial questions function quite similarly in that they jolt
the reader into registering the new stanzaic impetus. They are
more striking if they are very brief and occur in isolation. In
the first and third of the examples below, the initial emphasis
is supported by a rhythmical and visual device of pauses indicated by a dash.

> Yet why? – a silvery current flows . . .
> > (Wordsworth, 'Yarrow Visited', l. 9)

> Who hath not seen thee oft amid thy store?
> > (Keats, 'To Autumn', l. 12)

> Were they unhappy then? – It cannot be –

> Why were they proud? Because their marble founts
> Gush'd with more pride than do a wretch's tears?
> > (Keats, 'Isabella; or the Pot of Basil',
> > ll. 89, 121–2)

In the last example the effect diminishes, because the question turns out to be a new stanzaic norm. This is even more re-

markably so in Suckling's 'Why so pale and wan fond
Lover?', whose first two stanzas contain only questions.
Their stanzaic identity rests on the varying structure of the
questions ('Why . . . ?/Prithee why . . .?/Will . . ./. . .?/Prithee
why . . .?//) and the stanzaic parallels (see below, pp.80–1); the
question itself does not represent a departure from the expected norm but constitutes the basic principle. The mere recurrence of the basic principle of expectation, however, never
contributes to initial or closural emphasis and thus does not
suggest stanzaic unity.

Quotations placed at stanzaic openings may be employed
as such departures from the norm. In Vaughan's
'Regeneration' the speaker, who narrates the pursuit of his
soul's 'spring', responds to the command of an unidentified
voice:

> With that, some cryed *Away*, straight I
>   Obey'd, . . .   (ll. 25–6)

The quotation surprises the reader and thus effects initial emphasis. In the same poem the speaker rouses the reader's
attention by addressing him directly:

> The first (pray marke,) as quick as light
>   Danc'd through the flood . . .   (ll. 43–4)

The beginning of the stanza seems very suitable for this point
of special emphasis.

We have already noted the stanzaic relevance of emotional
heightening through exclamations, apostrophes and
expletives. Very frequently, these are linked to phrases
alluding to events that imply starts, beginnings and surprising developments. They are favourite devices of poetic
opening; their impact is heightened considerably if they occur
within the poem, because they usually initiate a new phase in
the poem's development:

> Wake, now my loue, awake; for it is time,
>> (Spenser, 'Epithalamion', l. 74)

> Awake, my lute, and struggle for thy part . . .

> The Sunne arising in the East,
>> (Herbert, 'Easter', ll. 7, 23)

> Arise sad heart; . . .
>> (Herbert, 'The Dawning', l. 9)

> And now in age I bud again,
>> (Herbert, 'The Flower', l. 36)

> When I begin to sing, begin to sound
> Sounds loud and shrill,
>> (Sir J. Wotton, 'Tune on my pipe',
>> ll. 11–12)

In Herbert's poetry these opening allusions amount almost to leitmotifs, which are intimately bound up with the central meaning of *The Temple*. The last quotation from Wotton involves another, less obvious feature of stanzaic opening, that of initial assonance (see the [i] and [au] sounds). With initial alliteration, euphony and cacophony, it belongs to a group of phonetic devices which too easily elude the visually preoccupied reader.

The vogue of 'hunting the letter' so prevalent among the sixteenth-century 'rakehellye route of . . . ragged rymers' (E. K.) can occasionally be traced in stanzaic openings. A poem by E. S. contained in *The Paradise of Dainty Devices* (1576), for example, utilizes different alliterative sounds in three stanzas:

> Why should I longer long to live

> The grass, methinks, should grow in sky,

The fish in air should fly with fin,
> (E. S., 'Why should I longer long to live,
> ll. 1, 13, 19)

Sidney seems to turn to alliteration for ironic effects:

Silvanus long in love, and long in vaine,
> (Sidney, *The Lady of May* 3, l. 1)

Poore Painters oft with silly Poets joyne,
> (Sidney,*Old Arcadia* 8, l. 1)

The lines by E. S. are, of course, infinitely more crude than the deftness of Sidney or the mellifluent harmony in Keats:

O Attic shape! Fair attitude with brede
Of marble men and maidens overwrought ...
> (Keats, 'Ode on a Grecian Urn', ll. 41–2)

Forlorn! the very word is like a bell
To toll me back from thee to my sole self!
> (Keats, 'Ode to a Nightingale', ll. 71–2)

Phonetic features operate so subtly and unobtrusively that we fail to notice them unless they are supported by other initial (or closural) devices. Their impact, however, is occasionally overrated, which has led to fanciful speculations like Dell H. Hymes's theory concerning summative sounds ('Phonological Aspects of Style. Some English Sonnets', in T. A. Sebeok (ed.), *Style and Language* (New York, 1960)).

We are on safer ground when dealing with word repetition. Correlative verse, a hitherto neglected phenomenon that was very popular in at least two centuries of English (and European) poetry (1500–1700), seems extremely relevant for stanzaic structure. Since the pioneer studies of Damaso Alonso and J. Fucilla fail to discuss the stanzaic implications of correlative verse, we shall stress these aspects in this chapter. The correlative unit, which contains all the members of a correlation, may be placed at different points of the poem. If the unit precedes the distribution (= dissemination) of the individual members, and if this unit is placed at the stanzaic opening, it attains a considerable degree of emphasis. One of the most ingenious attempts of this pattern we find in Herbert's 'The Call', which I quote in its entirety:

Come, my Way [A_1], my Truth [A_2], my Life [A_3]:
Such a Way [A_1], as gives us breath:
Such a Truth [A_2], as ends all strife:
Such a Life [A_3], as killeth death.

Come, my Light [B_1], my Feast [B_2]. my Strength [B_3]:
Such a Light [B_1], as shows a feast [B_2]:
Such a Feast [B_2], as mends in length:
Such a Strength [B_3], as makes his guest.

Come, my Joy [C_1], my Love [C_2], my Heart [C_3]:
Such a Joy [C_1], as none can move:
Such a Love [C_2], as none can part:
Such a Heart [C_3], as joyes [C_1] in love [C_2].

If it were not for the straitjacket of the rhyme scheme and the occasional *rime batelée*, there would be no need for the distribution of 'Way'–'Truth'–'Life','Light'–'Feast'–'Strength' in this sequence (ll. 2-4 and 6-8) because of the extraordinary self-sufficiency of these lines; even ll. 10 and 11 – the strong poetic closure caused by the recapitulated unit in l. 12 precludes the rearrangement of this line – could be placed at different points within the third stanza. The first lines of these three stanzas, which invariably contain the units of this three-membered triadic correlation, represent extremely forceful openings, which are clearly separated from the ensuing lines of dissemination both syntactically and rhythmically: even the caesuras of these lines are regular. The recurrent opening allusion 'Come' contributes to the amazing integrity of these stanzas, which is supported by phonetic and syntactic parallels and correspondences. In this poem, stanzaic unity does not depend on retrospective patterning, but is caused primarily by initial emphasis.

Stanzaic closure

Features of stanzaic closure may impress the reader more strongly than openings because they delimit stanzas *ex posteriori*. It is essential to realize that retrospective patterning is not only performed between several stanzas (see the section below) but also within individual stanzas. This distinction is valid, because we are isolating devices pertaining to individual stanzaic wholes and their degree of integrity. The fact, however, that stanzaic closure does involve retrospection explains the predominance of terminal over initial devices, although some of them may occur in both functions.

This holds, for example, for long and short closural lines (see above, pp. 45–6). The following examples should encourage the student to compare short and long line closures and openings. The attitude of poets towards the difference may be illustrated by the fact that there is no traditional stanzaic form with single short or long line openings with the possible exception of the *ritornello*, whereas we encounter fixed and fairly popular forms like the sapphic ode or the Spenserian stanza with short and long line closures.

> Hopeless immortals! how they scream and shiver,
> While devils push them to the pit wide-yawning
> Hideous and gloomy, to receive them headlong
>   Down to the centre!
>   (I. Watts, 'The Day of Judgement',
>   ll. 25–8)

> O who does know the bent of womens fantasy?
>   (Spenser, *The Faerie Queene*, I.iv.24)

O why should heauenly God to men have such regard?
(Spenser, ibid.   II.viii.2)

Loe see soone after, how she fades, and falles away.
(Spenser, ibid.   II.xii.74)

All things decay in time, and to their end do draw.
(Spenser, ibid.   III.vi.40)

The Adoneus of the sapphic is primarily a rhythmic closure which has been either exploited as such or imitated in English accentual verse (see the poems mentioned above, pp. 34, 37).

The effect of such short line pauses increases if they terminate a longer stanza, e.g. in Donne's 'The Canonization' ('So you will let me love', etc.), where the last word resounds throughout the poem. The same holds for short line closures in consistently isometric stanzas, e.g. 'Yet I love thee' in Herbert's 'The Pearl'. A very striking example may be found in Dowland's Air 'Weep you no more, sad fountains'; its closure consists of only one word ('Sleeping'), which is part of a repeated phrase. The melodic line also descends towards the end of each stanza and closes on two long-drawn half-notes. The short line in Dowland's 'Fine Knacks for Ladies', on the other hand, represents a tag taken from the previous line ('The heart is true', 'Of me a grain', 'Of no removes'), which is repeated twice in the melody. This type of closural recurrence, which is frequently employed in Elizabethan Airs (Campion's 'Shall I come sweet love to thee', 'My sweetest Lesbia'), may be described as a terminal refrain which is limited to a single stanza.

The long lines quoted from Spenser were chosen because they are self-sufficient syntactic units and contain various other closural features. The criteria concerning the closural impact of short lines (line length, relation to adjacent lines) may be applied to long line closures as well: the terminal weight of the alexandrine in Shelley's 'To a Skylark' appears to be considerably greater than in the Spenserian stanza, although some lines of 'The Skylark' can be split into two six-syllable halves, which thus accord with the first and third lines of this $a_6b_5a_6b_5b_{12}$ stanza. The examples by Spenser illustrate that closural force increases in accordance with the duration of the established norm, in this case ten-syllable lines. Generally speaking, stanzaic closure may be defined as a significant departure from an intra-stanzaically expected norm. This definition steers clear of the problematic division between devices of form and content which Morse Peckham has criticized in B. H. Smith's *Poetic Closure* (*Genre*, V (1972), p. 63).

All kinds of word repetition imply phonetic recurrence. Like stanzaic openings, stanzaic closures may be stressed by assonance, alliteration, euphony, etc., if they are used with unexpected frequency. The simplest phonetic closure would seem to occur in rhyme clusters at the end of stanzas, which make the reader aware of identical 'harmonic groups' (Henry Lanz). The couplets and triplets of single ababcc or ababccc stanzas are likely to disrupt the reader's expectation of continued alternate rhymes and thus give closural emphasis: an established pattern is abandoned. Similarly, closure may be strengthened by a sudden absence of rhyme such as in Herbert's 'Deniall', which symbolizes the speaker's emotional agitation. As the reader proceeds, he realizes that the rhymeless short line becomes a recurrent pattern, which is abandoned with a surprising rhyme at the end of the poem, a very effective and moving poetic closure. The reverse may be found in rhymeless poetry, e.g. the sudden rhymes in Allen Ginsberg's 'On Burrough's Work', ll. 7–8. Some poets are unusually skilled in, and aware of, the possibilities of rhyming. In 'Even-Song', Herbert closes the first stanza (l. 8) with an internal (leonine) rhyme, which is especially prominent because of the pun on 'Sun'–'Son'. In 'The Water-Course' two rhymes are printed as alternatives at the end of each final line: 'Life'–'Strife' in l. 5, 'Salvation'–'Damnation' in l. 10. These antonyms encompass man's existence and function both as harmonic groups, i.e. as mere *homoioteleuta*, and as centres of meaning.

We have already met with correlative units in stanzaic openings. If the disseminated members precede the summative unit within a stanza we a have a stanzaically limited 'disseminative–recapitulative' correlation (Fucilla) with powerful closure. This phenomenon has never been evaluated for its stanzaic relevance. Our examples illustrate a few more or less sophisticated types of correlative closure.

> Earth [A₁] with her flowers shall sooner heaven [A₂]
>   adorn;
>   Heaven [A₂] her bright stars through earth's [A₁] dim
>   globe shall move;
> Fire [A₃] heat shall lose, and frosts of flames be born;
>   Air [A₄], made to shine, as black as hell shall prove.
> Earth [A₁], heaven [A₂], fire [A₃], air [A₄], the world trans-
>   formed shall view,
> Ere I prove false to faith, or strange to you.
>   (Dowland's *Songs and Airs*, I, anon.,
>   'Dear, if you change', ll. 7–12)

The couplet effects considerable closural emphasis through the repetition of the concentrated four-membered unit in l. 5, which is supported by a change of the rhythmic pattern (caesuras). Our next example contains a four-membered unit (nouns) accompanied by another series of four correlated 'elements' (Alonso) (verbs), which recur together at the end of the stanza; only one additional member ('fail', a₃) is missing in the recapitulation:

> Dear [A₁] if you change [a₁], I'll never choose again;
>   Sweet [A₂], if you shrink [a₂], I'll never think of love;
> Fair [A₃], if you fail [a₃], I'll judge all beauty vain;
>   Wise [A₄], if too weak [a₄], moe wits I'll never prove.

Dear [A_1], sweet [A_2], fair [A_3], wise [A_4], change [a_1],
  shrink [a_2], nor be not weak [a_4];
And, on my faith, my faith shall never break!

This stanza demonstrates how much Renaissance poets liked
to work with recurrence. The ostensible structural monotony
is frequently intended to direct the reader's attention to the
non-identical elements, which may contain the essential
facets of meaning. The sixth line closing the preceding stanza
by means of word repetition marks the conclusion of an
extremely compact stanza. The reader will undoubtedly
realize that this stanza belongs to the poem in Dowland's collection of Airs; in fact, it is the first stanza of this twelve-line
poem. One is tempted to reverse the order of these two
stanzas because of the structural complications and other additional closural features of ll. 1–6. Could we not easily re-
arrange them?

Ben Jonson employs a stanzaically limited correlation in
'See the Chariot at hand here of Love', which contains two
units. The second three-membered one, which is subtly implied in the preceding dissemination of a seven-membered
unit, occurs at the end of the stanza in which the speaker
extols the qualities of Charis:

Have you seen but a bright lily grow
  Before rude hands have touched it?
Ha' you marked but the fall o'the snow
  Before the soil hath smutched it?
Ha' you felt the wool of beaver?
      Or swan's down ever?
Or have smelt o'the bud o'the brier?
      Or the nard in the fire?
Or have tasted the bag of the bee?
O so white! O so soft! O so sweet is she!
                (Jonson, 'A Celebration of Charis. Her
                Triumph', ll. 21–30)

This closure, which concludes the whole poem, represents a masterpiece of correlative and closural technique. It inspired Sir John Suckling to his superb parody 'A Song to a Lute'; we should note, however, that Suckling's first unit consists of only six members, and that – by repeating 'false' (a_3) – he lengthens the final line for closure's sake.

Occasionally, rhythmic and syntactic correspondences develop into consistently recurring norms. If such parallels cease at the end of the stanza, closural emphasis is attained, as in the following lines:

No love, to love of man and wife;
No hope, to hope of constant heart;
No joy, to joy in wedded life;
No faith, to faith in either part:
    Flesh is of flesh, and bone of bone
    When deeds and words and thoughts are one.
            (Eedes, 'No love, to love of man and wife'
            (1596), ll.1–6)

The two main sections of the stanza are distinguished syntactically: the quatrain consists of four identical lines hammering away the speaker's delight about 'the marriage of true minds'. The reader's expectation is clearly set up after the first two lines. The couplet, however, is likely to alert the reader who has already resigned himself to the prospect that this monotonous rambling could continue indefinitely – the tedious pattern resumes quickly enough in the next stanza. Since the couplet's import, like that of the preceding lines, is a commonplace, the departure from the syntactic parallels represents the only significant change within the first stanza. The reader may wish to compare the use of this closural device in Sidney's *Old Arcadia* 46 ('O WORDS which fall like sommer deaw on me').

Such a schematic treatment of stanzas is rare after 1700 or so. It may, however, be regarded as a touchstone for a poet's art and subtlety which later times chose to neglect. It may also be a touchstone for readers, who are called upon to discover minute effects of phonetic and rhythmical variations and occasionally hidden and unobtrusive elements of brilliant craftsmanship. Closural parallels at the end of loosely constructed stanzas function quite similarly to the device described above.

Another rhythmic feature involves the switch of metrical modes: a poem which begins trochaically presents distinct stanzaic closures if any of the last lines turns out to be iambic, dactylic or anapaestic.

> Onely joy, now here you are,
> Fit to heare and ease my care:
> Let my whispering voyce obtaine,
> Sweete reward for sharpest paine:
> Take me to thee, and thee to me.
> 'No, no, no, no, my Deare, let be.'
>
> (Sidney, *Astrophil and Stella*, iv, ll. 1–6)

Sidney changes the metrical base in the last two lines, which also form the refrain. Stanzaic closure arises from the urgency of Astrophil's wooing in l. 5, which is heightened by the metrical alteration. The change of speakers, the rhythmical idiosyncrasies of Stella's refusal, and the closural allusion 'let be' contribute to stanzaic unity and strong closure. Lines 5–6 recur in each stanza; they embody the gist of the poem – and the ironic reversal in the final lines (ll. 53–4). The combination of four distinct closural features in the first stanza reveals Sidney's superb stanzaic technique.

The change of speakers at the end of stanzas attains closural emphasis similar to quotations of various kinds, with which it is often identical. This device appears so often in Herbert that it may be regarded as one of his favourite and most conspicuous methods of stanzaic (and poetic) closures;

he never fails to underline quotations. The reader will recognize some biblical tags in the following examples:

Thy words were then, *Let me alone*.
('Decay', l. 5)

Man is but grasse,
He knows it, fill the glasse.
('Miserie', ll. 5–6)

Thou art still my God.
('The Forerunners', l. 6)

Lesse than the least
Of all thy mercies, is my posie still.
('The Posie', ll. 3–4, 11–12)

My joy, my life, my crown!
My heart was meaning all the day,
Somewhat it fain would say:
And still it runneth mutt'ring up and down
With onely this, *My joy*, *my life*, *my crown*.
('A true Hymne', ll. 1–6)

The first examples hark back to Exodus 32 : 10, Isaiah 40 : 6 and Psalm 31 : 14. In 'A true Hymne' the speaker introduces his prayer with an exclamation, which has been the heart's constant utterance during the whole day. This quotation is at the same time an intra-stanzaic refrain; furthermore, it is preceded by 'onely', which gives additional emphasis to the closure. The quotation may be called a self-quotation: the speaker refers to his own words spoken in the immediate or distant past.

One of the most remarkable instances of such quotations occurs in a poem attributed to Queen Elizabeth I. It has a refrain with significant rhythmic changes, short closural lines and words implying absolutes ('no more'); I quote the second

stanza, which provides some interesting hints for bio-
graphical speculations:

> How many weeping eyes I made to pine with woe,
> How many sighing hearts, I have no skill to show:
> Yet I the prouder grew, and answered them therefore,
>   'Go, go, go, seek some otherwhere!
>   Importune me no more!'
>
>   (Queen Elizabeth I, 'When I was fair and
>   young', ll. 6–10)

Closural emphasis is heightened if the speaker quotes
foreign words. A well-known example may be found in
Donne's 'Hymn to God my God, in my sicknesse', l. 10: '*Per
fretum febris*, by these streights to die'; despite the closural
allusion, closure seems to be weaker than the following lines
from Sir Henry Wotton's poem with a very similar title and
topic:

> O pretious Ransome! which once paid
> That *Consummatum Est* was said.
>
>   (Sir Henry Wotton, 'A hymn to my God
>   in a night of my late Sicknesse', ll. 11–12)

The outstanding closural force of this stanza arises from the
fact that the couplet is marked very strongly ('*O* pretious
Ransome!'), that Christ's words are quoted, and that these
words imply a very emphatic closural allusion since they refer
to Christ's death on the cross. Another striking example of
closural quotation occurs in the refrain of Byron's 'Maid of
Athens, ere we part': 'Ζώη μοῦ, σᾶζ αγαπῶ'.

Questions that are posed and answered within a stanza
may be regarded as a very similar type of closure, because
they involve a change of speakers or voices. In W. Davison's
'At her fair hands', the speaker engages in a complaint about

his obdurate mistress which develops into a dialogue with his heart at the end of each stanza. I quote the last but one stanza:

> But if the love that hath, and still doth burn me,
>   No love at length return me,
>   Out of my thoughts I'll set her.
> Heart let her go; oh heart, I pray thee, let her!
>   Say, shall she go?
>   Oh no, no, no, no, no!
> Fixed in the heart, how can the heart forget her?
>   (Davison, 'At her fair hands', ll. 29–35)

Whereas reason advises him to leave the lady, the heart staunchly contradicts such masochistic severity with a Sidneyesque 'Oh no, no, no, no, no!', which is followed by a counterargument. Question and answer are very brief and emphasize stanzaic closure. A more brilliant but differently structured instance of this device occurs in Ralegh's 'Description of Love', from which I quote the very witty third stanza:

> Yet what is love, I pray thee sain?
> It is a sunshine mixed with rain.
> It is a tooth-ache, or like pain;
> It is a game where none doth gain;
> The lass saith No, and would full fain:
> And this is love, as I hear sain.
>   (Ralegh, 'Description of Love', ll. 13–18)

The poem belongs to the vogue of Renaissance and baroque definition poems: the poet usually tries to characterize and illustrate the nature of the world, of life or of love by a string of images and correspondences. Very frequently, such lists develop into soporific catalogues. In strophic poetry the stanzaic units tend to disappear completely in a welter of details (see Ralegh's 'Farewell false love'). In 'The Description of Love' Ralegh skilfully avoids this danger by clear stanzaic boundaries: each of the five stanzas starts out with a question which also introduces the stanzaic rhyme. The answers are summarized ('And this is love') and revert to the stanzaic openings ('as I hear sain', etc.). This method of stanzaic framing strengthens the unity of this question–answer pattern considerably (see also next section).

It seems almost paradoxical that questions, which normally set up tensions and expectations, should occasionally serve as closural features. If a question refers to the unanswerable, or if it is a rhetorical one, it may operate as poetic (Yeats's 'Among School Children') or stanzaic closure which can be recognized as such within the stanzaic unit or even in the question itself. This is the case in the lines quoted from Spenser and Davison (see above, pp. 53–4, 62) and in the following passage from Southwell. If we attend to the next stanza, we realize that the question is practically answered in ll. 5–6 – or 'in between' the two stanzas:

> Though all the East did quake to hear
> Of Alexander's dreadful name,
> And all the West did likewise fear
> To hear of Julius Caesar's fame,
> Yet both by death in dust now lie:
> Who then can 'scape, but he must die?
>
> If none can 'scape death's dreadful dart,
> > (Southwell, 'Before my face the picture hangs', ll. 43–9)

In many cases closural questions are placed in several analogous stanzas before the final stanza sums up the answers to all of them. The unity of such stanzas depends on inter-stanzaic retrospection, which will be discussed below. Good examples may be found in Sir Henry Wotton's 'You meaner beauties of the night' and G. Fletcher's 'Say earth, why hast thou got thee new attire'.

Commonplaces belong to an extremely important group

of thematic closure: any succinct, proverbial, sententious, aphoristic, epigrammatic or summarizing statement at stanzaic endings results in closural emphasis. Again, such devices implying brevity, concentration and a certain 'catchiness' may have a more conspicuous and impressive effect in poetic closures. However, poets who tend to segment their lyrics stanzaically may also choose them for individual stanzas. If such devices are employed in several consecutive stanzas, the poem will be made up of a chain of distinct units which will shape its structure considerably. In Herbert's 'Dotage', for example, the short final lines summarize the preceding stanzaic survey of man's vanity and grief:

These are the pleasures here.

These are the sorrows here.
>   ('Dotage', ll. 6, 12)

These are then contrasted with the joys of heaven in the last stanza, which sums up the poem as a whole. The reader recognizes such summaries by demonstrative pronouns and adjectives, and by adverbial tags like 'so', 'thus', 'then', 'in sum', 'in short':

In short for to resound her praise,
She is the fairest of her days.
>   (*Bartlet's Book of Airs* (1606), 'Who doth
>   behold', ll. 5–6, 11–12, 17–18)

So I my Best-Beloved's am; so He is mine.
>   (Quarles, 'My beloved is mine', l. 6)

Then shall the fall further the flight in me.
>   (Herbert, 'Easter-wings', l. 10)

Thus are true Aarons drest.

Poor priest thus am I drest.
>   (Herbert, 'Aaron', ll. 5, 10)

Such Miracles are ceast; and now we see
No *Towns* or *Houses* rais'd by Poetrie.
(Cowley, 'Ode: Of Wit', ll. 31–2)

The line from Herbert's 'Easter-wings' derives part of its
effect from the paradox (*felix culpa*), which is a closural
feature in its own right. It may be grouped with surprise endings and hyperbolic expressions. The reader tends to ponder
such closures, because he is not gradually led to, but frequently shocked into, them. Such a sudden climax may be
called terminal heightening; this term has been defined as 'in-
creased movement, tension or interest in the last segment(s)'
by Paula Johnson, who fails to apply the concept to problems
of stanzaic unity. The structural differences may be observed
in the following stanza by Sidney (a typical example of Renaissance *gradatio*) and in the terminal heightenings in
poems by Surrey, an anonymous poet and Vaughan. Both
hyperboles and paradoxes are, of course, the stock-in-trade
of Petrarchan love lyrics; the example by Vaughan demonstrates the Metaphysical predilection for contrarieties and
coincidentiae oppositorum.

Who have so leaden eyes, as not to see sweet beautie's
show
Or seeing, have so wodden wits, as not that worth to
know;
Or knowing, have so muddy minds, as not to be in love;
Or loving, have so frothy thoughts, as easily thence to
move:
O let them see these heavenly beams, and in faire letters
reade
A lesson fit, both sight and skill, love and firme love to
breede.
(Sidney, *Astrophil and Stella*, 'Song vii',
ll. 7–12)

And virtues has she many moe
Than I with pen have skill to show.

And this was chiefly all her [Nature's] pain –
She could not make the like again.
>   (Surrey, 'Give place, ye lovers', ll. 11–12,
>   23–4)

These things seem wondrous, yet more wondrous I,
Whose heart with fear doth freeze, with love doth fry.
>   (Weelkes's *Madrigals*, 'Thulë, the period
>   of cosmography', ll. 5–6)

Most blest believer he! [Nicodemus]
Who in that land of darkness and blinde eyes
Thy long expected healing wings could see,
    When thou didst rise,
And what can never more be done,
Did at mid-night speak with the Sun!
>   (Vaughan, 'The Night', ll. 7–12)

The paradox of this last quotation is especially remarkable because the preceding lines develop the contrast of day and night; the reader is nevertheless surprised by the closure, which is announced in l. 11, and which culminates in the pun on 'Sun'–'Son'.

In didactic poetry we find proverbs, maxims, household quotations and common words of wisdom marking stanzaic closure. Many sixteenth-century poets seem to be fond of quaint – and often ridiculous – sayings, which usually appear in refrains. More sophisticated craftsmen have composed very effective closures of this type, which are frequently integrated into the rest of the stanza. The reader will notice that some topics lend themselves naturally to this device, e.g. the vanity and mutability of this world, of man and of love.

For wedding and hanging is destiny.
>> (Anon., 'I am a poor tiler' (1561), ll. 5, 10,
>> etc.)

The falling out of faithful friends, renewing is of love.
>> (Edwards, 'In going to my naked bed',
>> ll. 8, 16, etc.)

In all things that thou seest men bent,
See all! say noght! hold thee content!
>> (J. Heywood, 'If thou in surety', ll. 5–6,
>> 11–12, etc.)

Beauty, strength, youth, are flowers but fading seen
Duty, faith, love, are roots, and ever green.
>> (Peele, 'His golden locks time hath to
>> silver turned', ll.5–6)

Journeys end in lovers' meeting,
  Every wise man's son doth know.

Then come kiss me, sweet-and-twenty,
  Youth's a stuff will not endure.
>> (Shakespeare, 'O mistress mine', ll. 5–6,
>> 11–12)

We have already discussed the initial emphasis of allusions denoting beginnings. Closural allusions refer to events and actions implying permanence, stability, or the final stages of a stretch of time like death and decay, sleep and rest, night, peace, autumn and winter, heaven and hell, falls and descents, leavetakings and homecomings, and some ultimates like 'last', 'forever', 'no more', etc. The reader should note the frequent cooperation of various devices including closural allusions in the following examples:

For in your beauties orient deepe,
These flowers as in their causes, sleepe.

For in your sweet dividing throat,
She winters and keepes warme her note.
        (Carew, 'Aske me no more', ll. 3–4, 11–12)

To thee my sighs, my tears ascend:
        No end?
        (Herbert, 'Longing', ll. 5–6)

Sweet spring, full of sweet dayes and roses,
A box where sweets compacted lie;
My musick shows ye have your closes,
        And all must die.
        (Herbert, 'Vertue', ll. 11–12)

The stanza from 'Vertue' represents the terminal point of a development: both preceding stanzas teem with allusions to transience and death. The summative third stanza, which concludes the section by additional closure ('all'), is then contrasted with, and transcended by, the immortality of the soul in stanza 4 ('Then chiefly lives', l. 16).

Barbara H. Smith has called attention to the closural force of what she terms 'unqualified assertions': statements implying some kind of finality, 'the last word', as it were, on which there is no need to elaborate, statements which can not be further defined or qualified. Usually, we find universals and absolutes ('all', 'every', 'nothing', 'only', 'never', 'always', 'forever', etc.) and superlatives ('last', 'best', 'highest', 'most', etc.), which convey a sense of extremity and *Letztendlichkeit*. Since there are definitely more stanzas than poems concluded this way, it is disappointing that Smith did not realize the stanzaic implications of her observations.

Stanzaic closures of this type demonstrate how relative closural devices really are, because they in no way preclude the continuation of a train of thought. On the contrary, they may even serve as points of departure, as in Donne's 'Negative love' or Campion's 'Never weather-beaten sail'.

Although they may be strong closural features, they depend on the lines and stanzas surrounding them. As stanzaic closures, they provide a momentary standstill, a 'resting place' (Puttenham) at the end of a segment, from which the poem may carry on by developing previous implications or by going off in a completely different direction. This fact explains why we occasionally experience a fairly strong sense of poetic closure when a stanza is placed at the bottom of a page, although the poem continues on the next. It is not always due to the poet's incompetence that we are surprised at the poem's continuation, because a comparatively small number of poems contain definite and obvious tensions and stimuli whose release strikes the reader as absolutely inevitable at the final conclusion. Usually we determine retrospectively whether the main stimuli of a poem have been resolved, but there are many instances where there remain a great variety of potential stimuli, which might have been developed beyond poetic closure.

The reader should test this tenet by reading the following poems until he reaches the passages quoted below. We should try to determine whether the poems might not satisfactorily end there.

> If then at first wise Nature had
> Made women either good or bad,
>   Then some wee might hate, and some chuse,
> But since shee did them so create,
> That we may neither love, nor hate,
>   Onely this rests, All, all may use.
>   (Donne, 'Communitie', ll. 7–12, the second
>   of four stanzas)

> Fruits of much griefs they [the tears] are, emblemes of
>   more,
> When a teare falls, that thou falst which it bore,

So thou and I are nothing then, when on a diverse shore.

> (Donne, 'A Valediction: of weeping',
> ll. 7–10, the first of three stanzas)

Thou, when thou retorn'st, wilt tell mee
All strange wonders that befell thee,
  And sweare
  No where
Lives a woman true, and faire.

> (Donne, 'Song. Goe and catche a falling
> starre', ll. 14–18, the second of three stanzas)

  It cannot bee
That thou lov'st mee, as thou say'st,
If in thine my life thou waste,
  Thou art the best of mee.

> (Donne, 'Song. Sweetest love, I do not goe',
> ll. 29–32, the fourth of five stanzas)

Or if, when thou, the worlds soule, goest,
  It stay, tis but thy carkasse then,
The fairest woman, but thy ghost,
  But corrupt wormes, the worthyest men.

> (Donne, 'A Feaver', ll. 9–12, the third of
> seven stanzas)

  Only our love hath no decay;
This, no to morrow hath, nor yesterday,
Running it never runs from us away,
But truly keepes his first, last, everlasting day.

> (Donne, 'The Anniversarie', ll. 7–10, the
> first of three stanzas)

If we had only the first two stanzas of 'Communitie', 'Song. Goe and catche a falling starre', or four stanzas of 'Song. Sweetest love, I do not goe', the reader would not necessarily have the impression of fragmentariness. In 'Communitie' the second stanza very clearly resolves the potential stimuli of ll. 1–6: the speaker has stated the difference between good, evil and things indifferent, and explained man's attitude towards them. In the second stanza, he applies this distinction to women and proposes that – since they are things indifferent – all men may justly enjoy all available women 'as they shall find their fancy bent'. If the poem closed after l. 12, it would be more or less cynical, because in what follows the speaker sets out to prove why the fair sex is neither good nor bad, and nastily enlarges upon 'Onely this rests, All, all may use' in the fourth stanza. I do not mean to imply that we could easily do without the last two stanzas. The fact remains, however, that the stanzaic closure in l. 12 approximates to a very emphatic poetic closure. The continuation appears convincing *ex posteriori*, because we realize that the first two stanzas are well expanded and concluded in stanzas 3 and 4.

If we read the first stanza of 'The Anniversarie' and 'A Valediction: of weeping', we are hardly able to predict what kind of stimuli might successfully continue the poems. The stanza taken from 'The Anniversarie' is extremely well closed through the opposition between mutable and immutable love and the magnificent l. 10; the stanza does not point ahead to the discourse on death, afterlife and unparalleled dignity of love contained in the two succeeding stanzas. Modern readers might baulk at poems of one stanza; but what about the numerous examples in madrigal collections? Why are Ravenscroft's setting of the first stanza of Sidney's *Old Arcadia* 5, Youll's selection of the first stanza of *Astrophil and Stella*, 'Song iv', Byrd's setting of three and Dowland's collocation of stanzas 1–4 and stanza 8 of *Astrophil and Stella*, 'Song x', not mangled fragments but very pleasing poems? The answer is a hermeneutical one: many segments – like many everyday statements – convey some sense of closure which could be the final one if the inherent possibilities of their continuance were not taken up and developed. Very often, continuation is potential and may, or may not, be exploited.

Stanzaic framing

The initial and closural devices discussed so far cooperate in various ways to bring about stanzaic unity. In order to separate all these features we have as a rule excluded stanzas in which the same device appears as both opening and closure. The main difference of the following from all the preceding types resides in the fact that their stanzaic closures hark back to their openings, which leads to the effect of framing. Stanzaic unity through framing may be defined as the recurrence of a particular element at both intra-stanzaic boundaries. Strophic frames divide stanzas very clearly into three parts which are less obvious in stanzas exhibiting different opening and closural devices. Most openings and closures qualify for stanzaic frames except opening and closural allusions. Some frames hardly occur because poets prefer to use certain devices exclusively as openings or closures, e.g. summaries, switch of metrical modes, hyperboles, surprising statements, proverbs and epigrammatic sayings, universals and absolutes. Most of them are, however, theoretically possible as frames too. In what follows we shall concentrate on frames of short and long lines, rhyme clusters, syntactical and rhythmical parallels, emotional heightening, word repetition and internal refrain.

One form of framing we have already touched upon in discussing Ralegh's 'Now what is love' (see above, pp. 62-3), where initial words are taken up at the end of each stanza. This repetition, which can also be found in Wither's 'Shall I wasting in despair' among others, may be termed embryonic refrain. It is used most schematically in correlative verse, if the unit of all the members precedes their dissemination and a recapitulation at the end of the stanza.

Before tackling more sophisticated types we shall examine a few interesting but simple forms of framing. In reading the following stanza by Ben Jonson we should note the rhythm of the first and last lines:

Still to be meat, still to be dressed,
As you were going to a feast;
Still to be powdered, still perfumed:
Lady, it is to be presumed,
Though art's hid causes are not found,
All is not sweet, all is not sound.

Give me a book, give me a face, . . .
They strike mine eyes, but not my heart.
(Jonson, 'Still to be neat', ll. 1–6, 7, 12)

The first line is divided into two rhythmically identical
phrases of equal length (x̌xxx̌/x̌xxx̌), which are repeated
exactly in l. 6, at the beginning of the second stanza, and even
in the first half of the final line, which closes in a regular
iambic cadence. The frame is exceedingly subtle because it
rests on the recurrence of the caesura and the clash of stresses
in the centre of the lines. It is nevertheless audible,
although some other lines, notably ll. 3 and 4, invert the first
iambic foot, too.

An even more minute frame occurs in Donne's 'The
Expiration':

So, so, breake off this last lamenting kisse,
    Which sucks two soules, and vapours Both away,
Turne thou ghost that way, and let mee turne this,
    And let ourselves benight our happiest day,
We ask'd none leave to love; nor will we owe
    Any, so cheape a death, as saying, Goe;

Goe; and if that word have not quite kil'd thee, . . .
Except it be too late, to kill me so,
    Being double dead, going, and bidding, goe.
            (Donne, 'The Expiration', ll. 1–6, 7,
            11–12)

Donne utilizes a recurrent sound as frame; actually, it is similar to a framing rhyme, which we should include as such a device, especially when we find it in symmetrical stanzas, as in Anne Sexton's amazing 'Unknown Girl in the Maternity Ward'. In 'The Expiration' the position of the rhyming words at the very beginning and end of each stanza makes this instance a very unusual one.

George Herbert is justly famous for his handling of short and long line effects. One of his best-known poems, 'Easter-wings', as a virtuoso performance in long-line framing. The first of the two stanzas, which together form the wings of this pattern poem, describes the development from man's creation in 'wealth and store' (long lines) to the fall (gradually diminishing line length) to the soul's request (gradually increasing line length) and confidence that she will join in Christ's resurrection, and thus turn 'evil into good' (Milton), and damnation into grace and redemption (long lines). In both stanzas this use of long lines is emblematic. The same technique is employed in an instance of short-line framing:

> When God at first made man,
> Having a glasse of blessings standing by;
> Let us (said he) poure on him all we can:
> Let the worlds riches, which dispersed lie,
>   Contract into a span.
>   (Herbert, 'The Pulley', ll. 1–6)

The rhyme scheme $a_3bab_5a_3$ revolves around l. 3, the axis of symmetry, in which the Creator himself speaks, and which carries the stanza's central meaning: 'Let us . . . *poure* on him *all we can*'; the last line, which frames the stanza, imitates its words emblematically in that the line length is 'contracted'. Herbert has frames in 'Sunday' and 'Sighs and Grones' as well; from the latter I quote the following stanza, which combines about four framing devices:

>   O do not use me
> After my sinnes! look not on my desert,

But on thy glorie! then thou wilt reform
And not refuse me: for thou onely art
The mightie God, but I a sillie worm;
    O do not bruise me!
           (Herbert, 'Sighs and Grones', ll. 1–6)

Since these lines contain expletives, syntactic anaphora, rhythmic parallels and rhymes, they constitute an extremely solid stanzaic unity through framing, which approximates to a stanzaic refrain. The only difference between the two framing lines resides in the additional phonemes [b] plus [r] in 'bruise' as opposed to [j] in 'use'.

Herbert may have borrowed the idea from Wyatt, who employs short-line refrains very frequently. They usually consist of no more than four or five syllables. It is through such refrains that Wyatt's poetry strikes us as basically stanzaic in structure.

    Is it possible
    That any may find
   Within one heart so diverse mind,
  To change or turn as weather and wind?
    Is it possible?
        (Wyatt, 'Is it possible', ll. 11–15)

In all stanzas except the final one the first line is integrated into a long sentence; the framing line, which is isolated, closes the stanza by way of an echo. The more usual intra-stanzaic refrain in Wyatt does not consist of two corresponding short lines but of an initial tag, which is part of the first line, and an echo line. Wyatt favours this technique as poetic opening ('Blame not my lute', 'Lo, what it is to love!', 'In eternum I was once determed', etc.). In a few instances he employs it also in every stanza. The most prominent examples are probably the following ones:

    Disdain me not without desert
     Nor leave me not so suddenly,

Since well ye wot that in my heart
  I mean nothing but honesty,
    Disdain me not.

Refuse me not without cause why ...
  Refuse me not.

Mistrust me not, though some there be ...
  Mistrust me not.
      (Wyatt, 'Disdain me not', ll. 1–5, 6, 10, 11,
      15, etc.)

These lines illustrate most clearly what we mean by a framing refrain, because the frames are limited to one stanza each. In 'Forget not yet' the same frame recurs throughout the poem:

Forget not yet the great assays,
The cruel wrong, the scornful ways,
The painful patience in denays,
    Forget not yet!
      (Wyatt, 'Forget not yet', ll. 9–12)

In this poem, the refrain functions both intra- and inter-stanzaically (see next section). The individual stanzaic unit is extremely compact, because the three rhymed lines are framed by the same tag. The technique of framing reminds us of a stanzaic poem which is structured by framing refrains: the rondeau. We have seen that Wyatt introduced this form into English poetry. His refrains were certainly influenced by the rondeau. The framing refrain, which may ultimately go back to medieval *versus caudati*, may be said to create a rondeau effect. Stanzaic frames are not as rare as one might assume. They appear, for example, in Sidney's *Certain Sonnets* 7, where they resemble Wyatt's 'And wilt thou leave me thus', in *Certain Sonnets* 26, Donne's 'Lovers infinitenesse', John Clare's 'Now is past' and 'Love, meet me in the Green Glen', Swinburne's 'A Match', Dylan Thomas's 'And Death Shall

Have No Dominion' and W. S. Merwin's 'The Drunk in the Furnace'.

Stanzaic recurrence

Distinct stanzaic openings and closures as well as frames allow the reader to determine the integrity of individual stanzas without recourse to adjacent ones. So far we have dealt only with intra-stanzaic retrospection, by which stanzaic units may be perceived as such. Very frequently, however, preceding and following stanzas contribute to a single stanza's unity, which the reader can realize only through inter-stanzaic retrospection. In such cases our expectation depends on at least two consecutive stanzas. Since we are analysing the possibilities of stanzaic unity we have to differentiate these two principles of retrospective patterning, although they cooperate often enough. Inter-stanzaic retrospection establishes units which share certain features. These include stanzaic anaphoras, parallels of various kinds, recurrent rhymes, lines and other identical elements in adjacent or distant lines and stanzas. Poetic closure is frequently indicated by the termination of such devices. We shall now survey a few devices of inter-stanzaic recurrence.

Any kind of regular stanzaic alternation contributes to stanzaic integrity. In Cowley and Crashaw's 'On Hope', for example, we expect the continuation of alternating voices after the second stanza. In such dialogues, pairs of stanzas belong together. The reader may wish to compare Sidney's *Old Arcadia* 71 ('Yee Gote-heard Gods'), Herbert's 'Dialogue' and Ralegh's 'As you came from the holy land'.

Stanzaic catalogues may also imply recurrence if they contain stanzaic parallels. In Hunnis's 'A Nosegay', which is alluded to in *Hamlet*, iv.v.176–84, we expect that the enumeration of flowers will continue in every stanza. The first line of each stanzaic unit is usually enforced by alliteration ('*Lavender* is for lovers true', l. 17, etc.). The pendant to this initial enumeration can be found in Herbert's 'The Church-floore', where three abstract nouns ('Patience', 'Humilitie', 'Confidence') appear in the final lines of three stanzas. Such catalogues are, of course, very frequent in blasons praising a lady's beauty by distributing eyes, lips, hands, feet, etc., stanzaically; Sidney's *Astrophil and Stella*, 'Song i', is a magnificent example.

In Donne's 'The Expiration' stanzaic unity depends on both intra- and inter-stanzaic recurrence: Donne repeats the framing rhyme [ou] in ll. 7 and 12; this double frame is especially effective because of the *rime annexée* in ll. 6 and 7. In Ferrabosco's setting the initial anaphora of ll. 1 and 7 is completed by an additional 'goe', which emphasizes the stanzaic correspondences:

> Goe, goe, and if that word have not quite kil'd thee, . . .
>   (Donne, 'The Expiration', l. 7, Ferrabosco's setting)

The unifying effect is essentially the same, if the final line of a stanza is repeated as the first line of the next, which – if kept up for several stanzas – leads to 'crowns' of stanzas as in Herbert's 'Sinnes round'. The device may be fitly called 'La Corona', since it is most prominent in crowns of sonnets.

Stanzaic unity through anaphora occurs very often in airs, because their stanzas have to conform to one melody. Composers of airs, therefore, have favoured poems exhibiting stanzaic parallels. Since many Renaissance and baroque poets liked to construct analogous stanzas, scholars like Pattison, Weiss and Johnson have rightly contended that the poetry of these periods was largely written for music. If we examine the poetry of Dowland and Campion, we encounter stanzaic correspondences of considerable sophistication. A very unobtrusive instance occurs in the following lines from Campion's 'When thou must home to shades of under ground', where the music provides the vital clues to the parallels and directs the listener to the poem's central meaning:

> To heare the stories of thy finisht love,
> From that smoothe toong whose musicke hell can move:
>
> When thou hast told these honours done to thee,
> Then tell, O tell, how thou didst murder me.
>> (Campion, 'When thou must home to shades of under ground', ll. 5–6, 11–12)

Campion stresses 'smoothe' in l. 6 by a climactic whole on E flat, the highest note of the melody. The speaker assumes that the Orpheus-like quality of his mistress, which is responsible for his despair, will not fail to impress the shades in Hades. In the second stanza, the mournful 'O', which is embedded in a closural repetition, is placed in the same position and aptly reflects the lover's emotional state. We have touched upon a more obvious example of this type of correspondence in discussing the rhythmical identities of Jonson's 'Still to be neat, still to be dressed' (see above, p. 73).

The stanzaic unity of Herbert's 'Mortification', one of the most remarkable poems of its time, depends both on the sequence of the five ages, the stanzaic recurrence of certain features, and the two central rhymes 'breath' and 'death'; they echo the paradox of 'death in life', which is reversed to 'life in death' at the poem's terminal heightening. Stanzaic rhyme recurrence is used in an even more sophisticated manner in 'Aaron': the rhymes 'head', 'breast', 'dead', 'rest' and 'drest' represent a five-membered correlation, which appears in stanzaic dissemination. Thus stanzaic correlation constitutes the stanzaic units of this poem. From 'Aaron' we can also infer the close relationship between correlative verse and the sestina (see above, p. 41).

Both 'Mortification' and 'Aaron' exhibit tendencies towards excessive stanzaic analogy, which Smith has called 'paratactic structure' and Johnson characterizes as 'directional models' (Smith, *Poetic Closure*, p. 98; Johnson, *Form and Transformation*, p. 64). They are based on grammatical and structural parallels and recurrent words and phrases. Extreme consecutive analogy results in exceptionally solid and self-sufficient stanzaic wholes. Although there are many monotonous examples of stanzaic analogy, such structures are by no means confined to drab or 'silver' poetry. Two of the most famous examples can be found in nearly all anthologies: Carew's 'Aske me no more' and Suckling's 'Why so pale and wan fond Lover?', from which I take the following stanzas:

> Why so pale and wan fond Lover?
>   Prithee why so pale?
> Will, when looking well can't move her,
>   Looking ill prevaile?
>   Prithee why so pale?
>
> Why so dull and mute young Sinner?
>   Prithee why so mute?
> Will, when speaking well can't win her,
>   Saying nothing doo't?
>   Prithee why so mute?
>   (Suckling, 'Why so pale and wan fond
>   Lover?', ll. 1–10)

Each stanza follows the same grammatical structure:

l. 1: question directed at a male person showing the effects of a harrowing experience in love by sullen behaviour (in his looks, by silence)

l. 2: interjection 'Prithee' followed by the same question as in l. 1, repeating only one of two adjectives;

l. 3: question which is interrupted by a temporal and causal subordinate clause expressing the abortive wooing of a female by opposite behaviour (looks, utterance);

l. 4: completion of question and reference to the ill-founded hope for successful wooing through present behaviour (looks, silence);

1.5: repetition of l. 2 (internal refrain).

We can write the skelton of these two stanzas, which will help us to concentrate on the stanzaic differences; the points of divergence are indicated by a dash:

Why so — and — — —er?
Prithee why so —?
Will, when —ing well can't — her,
—ing — — —?
Prithee why so —?

Out of thirty-one syllables, there are only twelve – eight of them in ll. 1 and 4 – which are not repeated in the second stanza. The only structural departure occurs in the second line of stanza 2, where the second adjective is taken up instead of the first. All the other differences are semantic: 'pale and wan' versus 'dull and mute', 'fond Lover' versus 'young Sinner', 'looking' versus 'speaking', 'move' versus 'win', 'Looking ill' versus 'saying nothing', 'prevaile' versus 'doo't'; most of them belong to the semantic fields of 'looking' and 'speaking'. Both stanzas derive their individual unity from a network of internal and inter-stanzaic repetitions. The poem certainly is an extreme yet skilfully constructed and amusing example of stanzaic analogy. In the third stanza the directional model is abandoned, which underlines the very effective poetic closure.

4

Stanza and poetic structure

> But doesn't the character of the whole depend on, arise out
> of, the character of the parts?
>> (Denise Levertov, 'Some Notes on Organic Form'
>> (1965), Allen–Tallman (eds), p. 316)

Having established how stanzaic unity can be attained we
turn to the relationship of stanzaic units within the poem as a
whole, i.e. instead of dealing with stanzas as wholes we shall
now attend to their function as parts within the superior
whole of the poem. By investigating stanzaic interrelations
we are applying Elder Olson's structural approach to the
stanza. Stanzaic relationship depends on what James V.
Cunningham has defined as a 'system of propositions', i.e. 'a
determinate relationship of signs forming an element in a
composition consisting of successive elements of this nature'
(*Tradition and Poetic Structure* (Denver, 1960), p. 15). In
other words, we shall analyse the structure of stanzaic poems
by determining the *logical* relations among their stanzas,
which are regarded as basic units. Every unit embodies
various elements of meaning, trains of thought and inter-
acting logical drives, which constitute what members of the
Chicago School call the *dynamis*, i.e. 'the shaping cause', of
any structural segment. I prefer the term stimulus, which is
not loaded with Aristotelian connotations and involves the
reader and the poem. It is also a more general term than
'impetus', which denotes urgency of movement characteristic
of only one of the three following types.

Stanzaic mobility

Let us first examine Herbert's 'Vertue':

Sweet day, so cool, so calm, so bright,
The bridall of the earth and skie:
The dew shall weep thy fall to night;
> For thou must die.

Sweet rose, whose hue angrie and brave
Bids the rash gazer wipe his eye:
Thy root is ever in its grave,
> And thou must die.

Sweet spring, full of sweet dayes and roses,
A box where sweets compacted lie;
My musick shows ye have your closes,
> And all must die.

Onely a sweet and vertuous soul,
Like season'd timber, never gives;
But though the whole world turn to coal,
> Then chiefly lives.

In the first two stanzas, which follow a similar directional model, the speaker addresses the day and the rose. In spite of their beauty and excellence, they are subject to mutability. The same holds for the spring, whose special qualities reside in both sweet days and roses. This stanza sums up the preceding ones and could constitute a very satisfactory closure (see above, p.69). The fourth stanza contrasts the transience of days, roses and spring with the sweet, i.e. virtuous, soul's immortality. The relationship between stanzas 1–3, on the one hand, and stanza 4, on the other, is one of opposition. Poetic closure is heightened because previous stanzaic anaphoras, syntactic parallels, rhymes and the refrain are abandoned in the last stanza.

The opposition operates first and foremost between stanzas 3 and 4, since the former includes the initial stanzas. If we had only the last two stanzas, the poem would be a perfectly understandable poetic whole. The climax in stanza 4 is developed mainly out of stanza 3. The reader perceives the relation between these two terminal stanzas *ex posteriori*, i.e. stanza 3 does not logically refer to or necessitate its continuation; it does not give us any clues as to whether there will be any succeeding development. Thus stanza 3 carries a very self-sufficient stimulus, which is neatly concluded at its end, and which is taken up in the highly convincing climax of stanza 4. Let us call this type of stanzaic *dynamis* light-stimulus (L). It links stanzas that seem to be independent and fixes them in their position: stanza 4 must follow stanza 3; stanza 3 must succeed the first two stanzas, i.e. the final two stanzas could not be rearranged.

Does this also hold for stanzas 1 and 2? If one of them had not come down to us, would we stumble over logical gaps? If we exchanged them, would we destroy the continuity and thus the meaning of the poem? Obviously not. We can test this view by reversing the order of stanzas 1 and 2 in print. Perhaps we prefer the succession of 'Sweet rose' after 'Sweet day', but one could argue that the more specific detail (rose) introduces the poem very aptly because it could lead to the more comprehensive one (day). The fact that the two members of the correlation appear in the same order in l. 9 does not imply fixation because words as such do not constitute logical progression unless they are arranged hierarchically; very frequently the order of correlative members is inverted or altered; generally, correlative and logical relations between stanzas belong to different categories and should not be confused. Stanza 1 of 'Vertue' contains a completely self-sufficient stimulus that is not taken up and developed but repeated in stanza 2. The logical stimulus is stanzaically limited in both cases: there is no logical progression from stanza 1 to 2; the two units are logically unconnected and independent; their position is therefore not fixed; they are exchangeable stanzas which vary the same basic idea – mutability – through structural analogy. Since these two stanzas can be re-arranged, stanza 3 refers to, and could be linked with, either of them. It could, however, not intrude between them. The logical *dynamis* of the whole poem may be summed up in stanzaic terms: two exchangeable stanzas (E_2) are summarized in a preliminary climactic stanza (L_1), which in turn is developed by contrast in a very strongly closural stanza (L_1): $(E_2 + L_1) + L_1$.

The possibility of rearranging has occasionally been recognized before. Most of the remarks on poems such as Surrey's 'The Happy Life' (B. H. Smith, op. cit. pp. 100–2), Nashe's 'Adieu! Farewell Earth's Bliss' (F. P. Wilson, *Elizabethan and Jacobean* (Oxford, 1945), p. 57; Y. Winters, 'The Experimental School in American Thought' (1937), *Defense of Reason* (London, 1960), p. 31), Ralegh's 'The Lie' (Winters, op. cit. p. 31; D. Peterson, *The English Lyric from Wyatt to Donne* (Princeton, 1967), p. 238; B. H. Smith, op. cit. pp. 102–8, 215–17) or Carew's 'Aske me no more' (Smith and Johnson, see below) merely hint at the problem but fail to analyse it in terms of stanzaic relations. They realize aspects of stanzaic recurrence and analogy but neglect the logical relations. We have to bear in mind that there are poems with recurrent stanzaic directional models with or without logical progression; also, there are poems with or without stanzaic analogy that have exchangeable stanzas.

In order to clarify the implications of our theory we have to discuss further examples:

The marchante man, whome gayne dothe teache the Sea
Where rockes do wayte, for theym the wyndes do chase,
Beaten with waves, no sooner kennes the baye
Wheare he was bounde, to make his marting place,
    But feare forgott, and paynes all overpaste,
    Make present ease receave the better taste.

The laborer, which cursed earthe up teares

With sweatie browes, sometyme with watrie eyes,
Ofte scorching sonne, ofte clowdie darkenes feares,
Whyle upon chaunce, his fruite of labour lyes;
    But harveste come, and corne in fertill store,
     More in his owne he toyld he gladdes the more.

Thus in my pilgrimaige of mated mynde,
Seeking the Sainct in whome all graces dwell,
What stormes founde me, what tormentes I dyd fynde,
Who seekes to knowe, acquaintes hym self with hell;
    But nowe successe hathe gott above annoyes,
     That sorrowe's weight dothe balance up thies joyes.
           (Sidney, *Old Arcadia* 36)

This poem, which shares many features with its twin, *Old Arcadia* 37, has two exchangeable stanzas. The logical relationship of either stanza 1 or 2 to the terminal stanza is one of implicit example and application ('Thus'): the speaker illustrates the frustration and subsequent fulfilment of his quest for his mistress's favour by the adventures and hazards of two different walks of life. If this relation were explicitly stated by 'As' in the first two stanzas and by 'Thus' in stanza 3, the first two units would still be mobile although intimately connected with the final one by way of a strong-stimulus unifying the poem *a priori*. Like Herbert's 'Vertue' we could easily understand *Old Arcadia* 36 if one of the two exchangeable stanzas were missing, even though the 'stormes' in l. 15 would lack a point of reference if we had only stanzas 2 and 3. The principle of stanzaic mobility was obviously recognized by one of Sidney's imitators in the *Phoenix Nest* (1593), which was a collection in homage of Sir Philip:

When day is gone, and darknes come
    The toyling tired wight,
Doth vse to ease his wearie bones,
    By rest in quiet night.

When storme is staied, and harbor woon,
  The Sea man set on shore,
With comfort doth requite the care,
  Of perils past before.

When Loue hath woon, where it did woo,
  And light where it delites,
Contented minde, thenceforth forgets
  The frowne of former spites.

> (*The Phoenix Nest* (1593), ed. H. E.
> Rollins (Cambridge, Mass., 1931),
> pp. 84–5)

The third stanza of this rather pedestrian poem seems to be fixed in its position, although its connection with the preceding stanzas is not as conspicuous as in Sidney's poem. We do, however, realize that the experiences of 'the toyling tired wight' and 'The Sea man' are not on the same level as those of the lover. The poet has inverted the order of 'The marchante man' and 'The laborer'.

That the principle of stanzaic mobility was recognized by poets, copyists and editors can be seen from different versions of certain poems. Thus, Morley took stanzas 3–5 from Southwell's 'Marie Magdalens *Complaint* at Christ's Death' and inverted their order for his air 'With my love, my life was nestled'. The most famous example is Carew's 'Song':

Aske me no more where *Ioue* bestowes,
When *Iune* is past, the fading rose:
For in your beauties orient deepe,
These flowers as in their causes, sleepe.

Aske me no more whether doth stray,
The golden Atomes of the day:
For in pure love heaven did prepare
Those powders to inrich your haire.

Aske me no more whether doth hast,
The Nightingale when May is past:

For in your sweet dividing throat,
She winters and keepes warme her note.

Aske me no more where those starres light,
That downewards fall in dead of night:
For in your eyes they sit, and there,
Fixed become as in their sphere.

Aske me no more if East or West,
The Phenix builds her spicy nest:
For unto you at last shee flies,
And in your fragrante bosome dyes.

This poem exists in various versions: the five stanzas are arranged as 1–4–3–5 (excluding stanza 2), 2–3–1–5 plus a couplet (excluding stanza 4), 2–4–3–1–5, 2–3–1–4–5–6 (additional stanza), and 2–3–1–4–5–7 (different version of stanza 6; see Dunlap (ed.), pp. 263–5). The stanzaic analogy of all these stanzas rests on the following pattern: 'in each stanza something beautiful is lost, then rediscovered in the mistress' (P. Johnson, op. cit. p. 48). The different versions suggest that exchangeable stanzas can be dispensed with, and that other stanzas can be added *ad libitum*. The fact that there is an additional stanza after stanza 5 in two versions indicates that the poem's closure was not felt to be inevitable, although the fifth stanza, which is never missing, appears invariably near the end, and although the additional stanza strikes the reader as anticlimactic. Thus, stanza 5 does constitute poetic closure; but it is much weaker than some scholars contend: B. H. Smith claims that the poem 'concludes with a strong sense of climax, stability and repose' (op. cit. p. 180); Johnson thinks that the poem exhibits closural features which contribute to 'an extra surprise and satisfaction', and 'an emotional lift' (op. cit. pp. 48–9). Since the relationship between the closure and the preceding stanzas is important for the poem's structure, we should examine why they overstate their case:

1 It is hard to see why 'dyes' in the final line should be interpreted as a *double entendre* (Johnson, op. cit. p. 49): the Phoenix is female in Carew's poem. The verb contributes to closure because it is somewhat stronger than the closural allusions in 'sleepe', 'winters and keepes warme her note', 'sit, and there, / Fixed become'. On the other hand, the rose, the 'golden Atomes of the day', the 'Nightingale' and 'those starres' may be said to die – 'and rise the same', just like the Phoenix.

2 The Phoenix does not fly to a specific part of the mistress but 'unto you' (l. 19); with this, the last stanza departs from the stanzaic analogy (Smith, op. cit. p. 181); on the other hand, she will then reside in 'your fragrante bosome'.

3 Smith contends that 'at last' (l. 19) implies the final death of the Phoenix (op. cit. p. 181); since she also claims that the bird's death 'also involves the idea of rebirth' alluded to in the other stanzas (p. 180), 'at last' can hardly be said to contribute to closure because rebirth and 'transcendental permanence' within the lady are incompatible: if the Phoenix is reborn she has to fly back to her Paradise. I take it that 'at last' refers primarily to the end of the Phoenix's flight from Paradise, to which she will return after dwelling – not in Arabia – but in the lady until her rebirth; the bird will prefer the lady as her 'spicy nest' in the future. This reading accords with the preceding stanzas in that the particular phenomena are said to seek a new resting place (in the lady), which they prefer to their previous abode. While I think that Smith's reading is contradictory, I grant that 'at last' may be ambiguous; it certainly departs from the analogous pattern, but its closural force is not exceedingly strong because it may contain another, more subtle analogy to the preceding stanzas.

4 Smith adduces the modernized punctuation of R. G. Howarth's edition (*Minor Poets of the Seventeenth Century* (London, 1959), pp. 148–9) as closural feature, which makes her fall prey to a devastating misreading: true, there is a

comma after l. 19 in the standard source (Dunlap (ed.), pp. 102–3), which could imply closure through rhythmical departure; end-stopped lines do, however, also appear in ll. 3, 11 and 15. Even if l. 19 contained the only comma in this position, it would be erroneous to regard it as such: all the bb couplets – and most of the aa couplets – of this poem are syntactic units which should be read as run-on lines. If the reader should nevertheless be inclined to pause after l. 19, he would have to do likewise after ll. 3, 11 and 15. It seems irresponsible to base an argument on erratic printing or what Catherine Ing has called 'metrical punctuation' (*Elizabethan Lyrics*, pp. 83, 85): compositors of the sixteenth and seventeenth centuries frequently marked line endings with commas.

Our analysis shows that aspects of stanzaic and poetic closure have to be approached with considerable circumspection. The interpreter who is thoroughly convinced of his theory may easily lapse into a distorting explication. In the case of 'Aske me no more' it involves a misrepresentation of the poem's structure: the poem is hardly a series of analogous exchangeable stanzas plus strong closure ('terminal heightening'), but it verges on a structure consisting of five mobile stanzas. We may compare the poem with Kynaston's 'To Cynthia. *On the concealement of her beauty*', an imitation of 'Aske me no more', whose closure in stanza 7 is much more convincing.

A poem containing only mobile stanzas belongs to a different structural category. Whereas its individual stanzas are all tightly closed, the whole poem is basically open. All exchangeable stanzas can claim equal logical status within the whole. Stanzas may be added or taken away anywhere. Stanzaic variations could continue *ad infinitum* – or *ad nauseam*. There is no stimulus that bounds the series of usually analogous parts. Skilful poets will avoid the danger of extreme *stasis* and monotony inherent in this structural principle. However, poems containing only exchangeable stanzas are very rare. Nor is it surprising that such poems are usually relatively short. Most of the examples consist of only two stanzas, e.g. Sidney's *Old Arcadia* 25, Shakespeare's 'When daisies pied, and violets blue' and 'When icicles hang by the wall' (from *Love's Labour's Lost*), 'You spotted snakes with double tongue' (from *A Midsummer Night's Dream*), Dowland's 'Dear if you change', Weelkes's 'Thulë, the period of cosmography' or Daniel's 'Love is a sickness full of woes'. Shelley's 'The World's Wanderer' has three mobile stanzas, as does Tichborne's well-known 'Elegy, Written in the Tower before His Execution, 1586':

My prime of youth is but a frost of cares;
   My feast of joy is but a dish of pain;
My crop of corn is but a field of tares;
   And all my good is but vain hope of gain:
The day is past, and yet I saw no sun;
And now I live, and now my life is done.

My tale was heard, and yet it was not told;
   My fruit is fall'n, and yet my leaves are green;
My youth is spent, and yet I am not old;
   I saw the world, and yet I was not seen:
My thread is cut, and yet it is not spun;
And now I live, and now my life is done.

I sought my death, and found it in my womb;
   I looked for life, and saw it was a shade;
I trod the earth, and knew it was my tomb;
   And now I die, and now I was but made:
My glass is full, and now my glass is run;
And now I live, and now my life is done.

The poem's eighteen lines revolve around the maddening

paradox of death in life. The accumulation of syntactically
and rhythmically identical lines endows the poem with a harrowing thrust and power. The refrain prevents it from dis-
integrating into a series of disconnected exchangeable lines.

Poems without closure seldom contain more than three
stanzas, e.g. Southwell's 'The loppëd tree in time may grow
again' or Christina Rossetti's 'The Three Enemies. The
Flesh', which have four mobile stanzas.

So far we have discussed the structural differences of
poems containing exchangeable stanzas with or without
poetic closure: one or several fixed stanzas succeeding a series
of exchangeable ones involve terminal heightening, i.e. 'in-
creased movement, tension, or interest in the last segment(s)'
(Johnson, op. cit. pp. 70–1). As long as there are mobile elements there can be no climactic sequence in the strict sense of
the definition; poems exclusively composed of exchangeable
stanzas are totally open.

In a third structural type one or several stanzas precede a
series of mobile ones without closure. Such poems are also
open, but the exchangeable units refer back to their common
point of departure; its impact dwindles if it is followed by a
great number of mobile stanzas. Let us examine the following
poem by an anonymous author of the seventeenth century:

> Whilst we sing the doleful knell
> Of this princess' passing-bell
> Let the woods and valleys ring
> Echoes to our sorrowing;
> And the tenor of their song
> Be ding dong, ding dong, dong,
>   Ding dong, dong.
>
> Nature now shall boast no more
> Of the riches of her store,
> Since in this her chiefest prize

All the stock of beauty dies:
Then what cruel heart can long
Forbear to sing this sad ding dong?
   This sad ding dong,
      Ding dong.

Fauns and sylvans of the woods,
Nymphs that haunt the crystal floods,
Savage beasts more milder than
The unrelenting hearts of men,
Be partakers of our moan,
And with us sing ding dong, ding dong,
   Ding dong, dong,
      Ding dong.

This song, which is taken from the play *Swetnam, the Woman-Hater* (1620), starts out with a reference to the burial of the princess. The first stanza is fixed because it announces the theme and introduces the 'ding dong' refrain, which represents the 'doleful knell'. The second stanza could easily change places with the third because it refers to general Nature's mourning and extols the lady's beauty. It also has a modified refrain. The 'cruel heart' in l. 13 could also point back to 'the unrelenting hearts' in l. 20. Stanza 3 could follow the initial stanza as well because it exemplifies the ringing echoes of woods and valleys. The poem's structure depends on one fixed initial and two exchangeable stanzas. The poem as a whole, although basically open, does not disintegrate into a loose sequence of stanzas because of its shortness and the refrain. It also shows that this structural type is based on doubtful closure. Since the closural force of either mobile stanza does not exceed that of the other, the poem remains without poetic closure.

If we compare the preceding poem with Sidney's 'The marchante man', their structural differences look like this:

Anon:

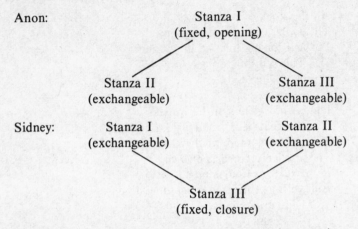

Sidney:

The structure of Ralegh's 'Now what is love', which contains fixed opening and closural stanzas, could be represented in the following manner:

Ralegh:

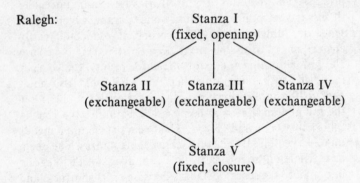

Let us analyse this poem more thoroughly:

Now what is love, I pray thee tell?
It is that fountain and that well
Where pleasure and repentance dwell.
It is perhaps that sauncing bell

That tolls all into heaven or hell:
And this is love, as I hear tell.

Yet what is love, I pray thee say?
It is a work on holy day.
It is December matched with May,
When lusty bloods in fresh array
Hear ten months after of the play:
And this is love, as I hear say.

Yet what is love, I pray thee sain?
It is a sunshine mixed with rain.
It is a tooth-ache, or like pain;
It is a game where none doth gain;
The lass saith No, and would full fain:
And this is love, as I hear sain.

Yet what is love, I pray thee say?
It is a yea, it is a nay,
A pretty kind of sporting fray;
It is a thing will soon away;
Then take the vantage while you may:
And this is love, as I hear say.

Yet what is love, I pray thee show?
A thing that creeps, it cannot go;
A prize that passeth to and fro;
A thing for one, a thing for mo;
And he that proves must find it so:
And this is love, sweet friend, I trow.

The poem's structure depends on very subtle departures from the directional model. The first stanza cannot be rearranged because its first line contains an introductory 'Now'; whereas stanzas 2–4 resound with an [ei] rhyme, stanzas 1 and 5 are based on different rhymes – [ell] and [ou]. Stanza 3, which has the rhyme [ein], would be the axis of symmetry if it exhibited any further central characteristics. It could take the place of both the preceding and the following stanza: it would, for example, be tempting to let ll. 16–17 precede the stanza containing ll. 10–11, which would result in an implicit sequence. The fourth stanza, which also alludes to plays and games, might also be placed before stanzas 2 and 3: the 'yea' and 'nay' would then precede the halfhearted rejection of the lover, which might nevertheless lead to unexpected consequences of the game within ten months. The mobility of stanzas 2–4 arises from the fact that neither the present nor any other arrangement is the more convincing one. The poem's rhymes in a sense mirror the structure of the whole, which consists of a frame. The tag 'sweet friend' in the final line lends closural weight to the last stanza. The line style of this poem appears to be very different from Tichborne's 'Elegy' because of the framing within individual stanzas. Ralegh's 'Now what is love' is a masterpiece of stanzaic and poetic framing. It is structurally superior to his 'Farewell, false Love', which is constructed according to the same formula: $L_1 + E_3 + L_1$.

We are now in a position to survey the structural implications of the basic types involving fixed and mobile stanzas:

1 One or several fixed opening stanzas precede several mobile ones $(L + E)$.
2 Several mobile stanzas are followed by one or several fixed closural stanzas $(E + L)$.
3 One or several fixed opening stanzas precede several mobile ones which are terminally heightened by one or several fixed closural stanzas (framing: $L + E + L$).
4 One or several exchangeable stanzas precede one or several fixed ones which are followed by one or several mobile stanzas $(E + L + E)$.

The fourth type is logically possible but even less frequent than $L + E$. I have found only two – atrocious – examples by Proctor and J. Heywood. Most poets tend to employ closed structures. It is difficult to judge whether open structures were deliberately planned as such before the anti-closural trends of our time; early examples of open form betray technical incompetence and insufficient awareness of the means of poetic closure. Modern poets, on the other hand, have not exploited openness stanzaically. I know of no open poem of the twentieth century that is based on exchangeable stanzas. In modern poetry, open forms are usually composed of variously linked stanzaic or non-stanzaic units, which somehow tend to peter out or simply avoid terminal devices.

The second and third types can be found rather frequently; in fact, they occur more often than one would suspect; nor are they confined to earlier, stanzaically more conscious periods. Sequences of two or three mobile stanzas plus one fixed closural stanza can be found surprisingly often, e.g. in Donne's 'The Message', 'The Prohibition', Suckling's 'Why so pale and wan fond Lover', Herbert's 'The Call', Keats's 'Stanzas. In a drear-nighted December', Browning's 'One Way to Love' and D. G. Rossetti's 'Love-Lily' $(E_2 + L_1)$, or Sir Henry Wotton's '*On his Mistris*, the Queen of Bohemia', Herbert's 'Vanitie (I)', 'The Pearl', Lovelace's 'To Althea, from Prison', T. Hood's 'The Autumn is Old', E. E. Cummings's 'All in green my love went riding' (three ten-line units plus five-line closure) and Dylan Thomas's 'The Force that through the green fuse drives the flower' $(E_3 + L_1)$, to name only a few famous examples. Poems comprising more than three mobile stanzas are less frequent. Owing to our increasing expectation of continuance and recurrence, the closure of such poems as Ogden Nash's 'Never Fair Weather' $(E_4 + L_1)$, Herbert's 'The Invitation' $(E_5 + L_1)$ or Herrick's 'A Ternary of Littles' $(E_6 \times L_1)$ seems rather sudden. In all these $E + L$ structures, closure is usually attained by significant departures from the expected inter-stanzaic norm or analogy. The impact of mobile units depends very much on their number and the force of closural stanzas.

The effect of exchangeable units decreases if they precede several fixed ones. As we can see in Herbert's 'Vertue', Blake's 'I love the jocund dance' ($E_3 + L_2$), D. G. Rossetti's 'Il Penumbra' ($E_4 + L_2$) and James Stephens's 'Sarasvati' ($E_2 + L_2$), the last but one stanza usually functions as preliminary terminal heightening that is taken up and completed in the poem's closure.

The main difference between $E + L$ structures and frames ($L + E + L$) resides in the strong initial and closural emphasis of the latter. Sometimes the framing stanzas are fixed because they contain features which make them more impressive than the others, as in Herbert's 'Unkindnesse' ($L_1 + E_3 + L_1$). The poet can also repeat the most important parts of the introductory stanza as in Wyatt's 'And wilt thou leave me thus' ($L_1 + E_2 + L_2$); Sidney even repeats the whole first stanza of *Astrophil and Stella*, 'Song i', at the end of the poem; the verbs of 'Onely in you my song begins and endeth' receive a different twist and emphasis in the final stanza: 'begins' is more prominent in l. 4; 'endeth' implies closure in l. 36.

The last stanza can also draw a forceful conclusion from preceding stanzas which have evolved out of a general statement of the poem's opening, such as in Nashe's 'Adieu! Farewell Earth's Bliss!' ($L_1 + E_4 + L_1$) or Donne's 'A Valediction: of the booke' ($L_3 + E_3 + L_1$). This pattern of general statement/ enumeration of details/conclusion is most characteristic of frames. Occasionally the catalogue starts in the initial fixed stanza, as in Donne's 'The Will' ($L_1 + E_3 + L_2$), where it continues into the closural stanzas. Consequently, only parts of the fixed stanzas function as frame; stanzaic units are not very strongly demarcated in the frame of such structures.

If a long poem contains a few mobile units, the term frame does not seem to be appropriate, e.g. for Shelley's 'To a Skylark', ll. 36–56, or for *Adonais*, stanzas 40–3. Such stanzas are mainly intended to provide structural variety.

Shelley's *Mask of Anarchy* does, however, have what we could call internal frames, because ll. 156–96, 209–53 and 299–330 represent important subordinate parts of the poem, in which several stanzas can be rearranged. Allen Ginsberg's 'Howl. For Carl Solomon I' shows that our concept of stanzaic structure applies equally well to other types of units: most of these Whitmanesque paragraphs in 'litany form' (Ginsberg) may be regarded as mobile parts within this otherwise amorphous agglomeration of details.

Exchangeable stanzas are usually independent units within a series or catalogue, or within a set of variations. Such structures are frequently employed in love poetry, notably in blasons, complaints and definition poems. Stanzaic mobility also appears in religious and didactic poetry; we recall stanzaic catalogues illustrating mutability or moral tenets. Although Dr Johnson does not refer to stanzas, the following observation shows that he was well aware of the structural principle of mobility in didactic poetry:

> Almost every poem, consisting of precepts, is so far arbitrary and immethodical, that many of the paragraphs may change places with no apparent inconvenience: for of two or more positions, depending upon some remote and general principle, there is seldom any cogent reason why one should precede the other.
>
> (*Lives of the English Poets*, 'Life of Pope',
> ed. G. B. Hill (Oxford, 1905), III, p. 99)

Although I do not agree with his charge of arbitrariness, Johnson has certainly hit upon something very important. Our examples have shown that poets utilized the principle deliberately, if not methodically.

Exchangeability should not be confused with repetition and analogy, although they sometimes coincide. Stanzaic mobility is a structural principle in its own right, which involves a lack of logical progression, inter-stanzaic *stasis* and extreme stanzaic self-sufficiency. Even if it occasionally entails monotony, it is by no means inferior to other structural principles.

Stanzaic progression

Stanzaic progression is certainly the predominant type of stanzaic relation. We have already seen that it may come about through the linked light-stimuli of syntactically closed stanzas. Linkage of this sort cannot be predicted because it is perceived *ex posteriori*. The following examples illustrate the difference between the light-stimuli and a third type of stanzaic relation which also involves progression.

> Little think'st thou, poore flower,
>   Whom I have watch'd sixe or seaven dayes,
> And seene thy birth, and seene what every houre
> Gave to thy growth, thee to this height to raise,
> And now dost laugh and triumph on this bough,
>   Little think'st thou
> That it will freeze anon, and that I shall
> To morrow finde thee falne, or not at all.

> Little think'st thou poore heart
>   That labour'st yet to nestle thee,
> And think'st by hovering here to get a part
> In a forbidden or forbidding tree,
> And hop'st her stiffenesse by long siege to bow:
>   Little think'st thou,
> That thou to morrow, ere that Sunne doth wake,
> Must with this Sunne, and mee a journey take.
>   (Donne, 'The Blossome', ll. 1–16)

> As virtuous men passe mildly away,
>   And whisper to their soules, to goe,
> Whilst some of their sad friends doe say,
>   The breath goes now, and some say, no:

So let us melt, and make no noise,
  No teare-floods, nor sigh-tempests move,
T'were prophanation of our joyes
  To tell the layetie our love.

> (Donne, 'A Valediction: forbidding
> mourning', ll. 1–8)

In both poems the stanzas are linked: the first stanza re-presents an example or simile which is applied to the speaker's situation in the second. The first stanza of 'A Valediction: forbidding mourning' indicates the connection by 'As'; since it does not include the application, we expect the continuation of the simile in stanza 2. The first stanza, which is syntactically open, fixes the second in its position. It predetermines the direction of the stimulus in the following unit, i.e. the stimulus is not limited to one stanza but carried over into the next. Since the stanzas are related *a priori*, we can call their stimulus a strong-stimulus.

The stanzaic relationship in 'The Blossome', on the other hand, can be recognized only retrospectively: in this poem, stanza 1 is perfectly closed and self-sufficient. The poem starts out like a dirge on the mutability of natural phenomena; it could very well continue in the vein of Herrick. The second stanza develops the first by using it as a point of departure for a valediction poem. Since we have no clue in the first stanza as to how the following stanza will carry on, its position is determined *ex posteriori*, i.e. a stimulus of stanza 1 is taken up in a way which we realize only in stanza 2. (If there were another example similar to the 'poore flower', we would have two mobile units related to a fixed third unit just as in Sidney's *Old Arcadia* 36!) If the following stanzas are connected by succeeding light-stimuli, the poem exhibits the structure of a chain of consecutive logical links.

Retrospective linkage

We should examine the main possibilities of linkage through light-stimulus. The first stanza of a poem is fixed in its position if it is not followed by stanzas of identical logical status. As initial stanza it introduces the theme, the main *personae*, etc., and sets the tone, e.g. in Ralegh's 'Now what is love', Wyatt's 'And wilt thou leave me thus' and Sidney's *Astrophil and Stella*, 'Song i'.

Very frequently a stanza elucidates aspects of the preceding one. The logical relationship is one of general statement and concretization or particularization. The first and the second, and the second and the third stanzas of Wordsworth's 'I wandered lonely as a cloud' are dependent on each other in this fashion. Conversely, a stanza can sum up the preceding one(s) by way of generalization, e.g. the last stanza of 'She dwelt among the untrodden ways'.

A stanza can also furnish an alternative to a preceding statement, such as the second stanza of Donne's 'Lovers infinitenesse'. Sometimes alternatives are introduced by 'and'; like 'too' and 'also', 'and' can link stanzas by adding on to something, as in the last stanza of Donne's 'The Canonization' ('And thus invoke us . . .'). Very often sequential relations are effected through such connectives. This type of linkage has been employed most subtly. Different stanzas can mark the stages of a development, as in Donne's 'The Expiration', or the stages of a temporal sequence, as in Herbert's 'Mortification', where this is especially conspicuous because of the stanzaic analogy. The development may depend on well-known patterns like 'give and take', as in Habington's 'To Castara. Give me a heart'. Sometimes the stages are numbered (first, second, third, etc.) or introduced as such (then, next, at length, finally), as in Herbert's 'Peace'. This kind of linkage is particularly effective if the sequence involves gradual intensification, which sometimes appears as stanzaic *gradatio*. An extreme example of such a climactic sequence is Sidney's *Astrophil and Stella*, 'Song v', ll. 43–84: in each of the seven stanzas the speaker upbraids his mistress by using a stronger epithet which is evolved out of the repetition of the preceding one: thief, murdering thief, tyrant, rebel, vagabond, witch and devil. Poems like Herbert's 'Sighs and Grones' or D. G. Rossetti's 'The Shadows' demonstrate the climactic force of this type. Stanzaic comparisons exhibit similar if more obvious characteristics of progression. The speaker of Wordsworth's 'She was a phantom of delight' refers back to l. 2 ('When first she gleamed upon my sight') at the beginning of the second stanza: 'I saw her upon nearer view'. Comparisons usually occur in sequences implying some hierarchy or order.

One or several stanzas can also be connected by logical inference and conclusion, a feature that appears very frequently towards poetic closure, as in Herbert's 'Deniall', ll. 21 and 26. The strongest and most frequent linkage through light-stimulus involves stanzaic contrasts; in highly argumentative poetry they tend to shape the structure of the whole to a considerable extent, as in Herbert's 'The Priesthood'. The same holds for causal relations. In Yeats's 'Sailing to Byzantium' the third stanza develops a purpose out of the second; this connection is as rare as concessive relations.

Finally, we also encounter stanzas that contain references to nouns. Such references can be personal and demonstrative pronouns and adjectives, place and time relations, etc. If they point backwards they fix the preceding stanza *ex posteriori*: the first two stanzas of Edward Thomas's 'The Gallows', which follow the same directional model, are prevented from being exchangeable only because of 'this keeper' in l. 11, which refers to 'a keeper' in l. 3.

All these relations represent the basic elements of poetic structure. The structure of light-stimulus poems depends on the force of such implicit or explicit relations, and on various

modes of cooperation between them. The following analyses
illustrate the nature of light-stimulus progression.

> Holinesse on the head,
> Light and perfections on the breast,
> Harmonious bells below, raising the dead
> To leade them unto life and rest:
> Thus are true Aarons drest.
>
> Profanenesse in my head,
> Defects and darknesse in my breast,
> A noise of passions ringing me for dead
> Unto a place where is no rest:
> Poore priest thus am I drest.
>
> Onely another head
> I have, another heart and breast,
> Another musick, making live not dead,
> Without whom I could have no rest:
> In him I am well drest.
>
> Christ is my onely head,
> My alone onely heart and breast,
> My onely musick, striking me ev'n dead;
> That to the old man I may rest,
> And be in him new drest.
>
> So holy in my head,
> Perfect and light in my deare breast,
> My doctrine tun'd by Christ, (who is not dead,
> But lives in me while I do rest)
> Come people; Aaron's drest.
>> (Herbert, 'Aaron')

The stanzaic analogy of this poem, which contributes so
much to the unity of the individual stanzas, accentuates the
logical development between them. Since the rhyme words remain identical throughout, the reader's attention focuses on

the beginning of every line. The first stanza describes the (outward) features of the true priest. In the second stanza the speaker reveals that he himself is made of 'Profanenesse', 'Defects and darknesse' and disharmonious passions, i.e. the second stanza develops a contrast between 'true Aarons' and this 'Poore priest'. Since the contrast resides in every line, the stanzaic connection is very strong. It also indicates the essential difference between Aaron, the Old Testament type of Christ, and the New Testament concept of priesthood ('on' versus 'in'). In the third stanza the speaker introduces another contrast: he can attain true priesthood by dint of 'another head', 'another heart and breast' and 'another musick'. In the next stanza, he explains his reference to 'another': Christ will extinguish 'the old man' in this priest and remake him in Aaron's and His own image. This stanza provides an implicit reason for l. 15 and initiates the poem's climax. It qualifies and intensifies l. 13 by alluding to the speaker's rebirth through grace, and by heightening 'well drest' to 'new drest'. The last stanza summarizes the whole. The logical relation to the previous stanzas is based on explicit inference ('So'); a new Aaron is portrayed, who can now address his congregation. The following paraphrase charts the stanzaic progression of this poem:

1 True Aarons are holy and full of God's light and perfections;
2 but I am destitute of all these qualities.
3 Yet there is somebody I can turn to;
4 for Christ will endow me with the necessary gifts of grace to 'make me new'.
5 Therefore I am now holy and full of God's light and perfections, and can fulfil the sacred office in Christ.

Donn's 'A Feaver' exhibits various other types of light-stimulus relation and illustrates the options a poet has in developing stanzaic progression:

Oh doe not die, for I shall hate
    All women so, when thou art gone,
That thee I shall not celebrate,
    When I remember, thou wast one.

But yet thou canst not die, I know;
    To leave this world behinde, is death,
But when thou from this world wilt goe,
    The whole world vapors with thy breath.

Or if, when thou, the world's soule, goest,
    It stay, tis but thy carkasse then,
The fairest woman, but thy ghost,
    But corrupt wormes, the worthyest men.

O wrangling schooles, that search what fire
    Shall burne this world, had none the wit
Unto this knowledge to aspire,
    That this her feaver might be it?

And yet she cannot wast by this,
    Nor long beare this torturing wrong,
For much corruption needfull is
    To fuell such a feaver long.

These burning fits but meteors bee,
    Whose matter in thee is soone spent.
Thy beauty, and all parts, which are thee,
    Are unchangeable firmament.

Yet t'was of my minde, seising thee,
    Though it in thee cannot persever.
For I had rather owner bee
    Of thee one houre, then all else ever.
        (Donne, 'A Feaver')

In the first stanza the speaker implores his lady, who has
contracted a fever, not to die. Donne develops only the first

four words of the poem in stanza 2; the rest of the first stanza consists of hyperbolical expostulations. In stanza 2 the lady's imminent death appears as false surmise. The stanzas are related through explicit contrast ('But yet'). Again the speaker adduces some hyperbolical reasons, this time to support his assertion that the lady is immortal; he implies that the world and his mistress are inseparable. If she left the world nothing at all would remain of it. The relevance of this argument becomes clear in stanza 3, which poses an alternative to ll. 7–8. The notion of the *anima mundi* is already alluded to in these lines. The third stanza approaches the same assertion from a different angle: if the lady left the world, its esemplastic power would be removed, and the drossy *materia* would stay behind in various shapes. The fourth stanza marks a preliminary climax, because it sums up the whole argument and is related to the preceding stanzas by way of implicit inference: the speaker concludes that he has hit upon the cause of the world's eventual conflagration. The poem could end satisfactorily on the hyperbolical note of this stanza. The speaker enlarges upon all this and continues with a sequential contrast. These links, which are supported by a demonstrative reference ('this'), operate mainly between ll. 16 and 17. The speaker qualifies his statement that implies the lady's destruction and reasserts her immortality: her fever could not last unless she contained a considerable amount of combustible dross. Since this is not the case the speaker has to cast around for another adequate way of defining the fever. It is therefore characterized as meteoric fire that will expire shortly.

The sixth stanza is thus linked to the previous one by allusions (ll. 19, 22), demonstrative reference ('These') and by implicit inference. At the same time, the stanza specifies several features of the lady's immortality. The fever appears as something extraneous, a sign of mutability that cannot really touch the lady. The last stanza is connected by another contrast and represents the speaker's final solution of his problem: the fever is described as his mind's encroachment upon the lady, his clandestine attempt to gain possession of her, however briefly. By implication, the speaker's mind appears as material and evanescent; at the same time it seems miraculously powerful, although it does not accord with the lady's immortality. The poem ends with a fantastic overstatement, which chimes with the rhetoric of praise pervading the whole. The argumentative movement of 'A Feaver' arises from the speaker's attempts to define the ailment of his mistress hyperbolically. In this piece of wit, Donne isolates certain elements of each stanza, which are subsequently developed. The reader has no clue in any stanza as to which of its stimuli will be taken up in the next unit. He could pause after almost every stanza and still make sense of the preceding 'fragment'. If we had only the first two or three stanzas it is doubtful whether we should have to regard them as torsi, because the light-stimuli of each stanza provide satisfactory closure. Interestingly, the opening lines of most stanzas are most instrumental in continuing the preceding light-stimuli; these lines emphasize the unity of their stanzas. This does not hold for the fourth and for the final stanzas, which determine the poem's structure most decisively. The poem's logical progression can be summed up as

introduction – explicit contrast – alternative plus connecting allusions – implicit inference and summary – sequential contrast plus demonstrative reference – implicit inference plus demonstrative reference and connecting allusions – explicit contrast plus pronoun reference and climactic overstatement.

We notice that these light-stimuli do not exhibit the same linking force: the alternative, the seqential contrast, and the demonstrative reference in stanzas 3, 5 and 6 are less impressive and obvious than the contrast of stanzas 2 and 7. The larger segments of the poem (stanzas 1–4 and 5–8) are accentuated by stimuli of different strength and by a combination of several stimuli. It is also remarkable that the number of light-stimuli that cooperate in linking stanzas increases towards the end of the poem. This may indicate that Donne tried to structure the conclusion tightly and convincingly, and that he wanted to avoid the impression of logical inconsistency and aimlessness.

Retrospective linkage is, of course, not limited to syntactically isolated stanzas. Subsequent stanzas can be attached to self-sufficient ones by way of various kinds of zeugmatic connections, non-defining relative and participle clauses, and subordinate clauses that are separated from their main clauses by stanzaic boundaries. In such cases, the position of the preceding stanza is fixed, and its syntactic and logical integrity is preserved. One or several stanzas may be linked that are syntactically dependent but logically closed. The essential feature of all light-stimulus connections holds for such links as well: the progression can in no way be predicted from the preceding fixed stanzas and is not realized as such except *ex posteriori*. The logical steps remain stanzaic units.

Linkage a priori

The logical integrity of a stanza tends to disintegrate if stanzaic links can be anticipated. The first stanza of Donne's 'A Valediction: forbidding mourning' contains a stimulus that points ahead, and that determines the logical direction of the subsequent stanza; thus their mutual relationship is predictable. The structural implications of such stimuli are important, because *a priori* links are basically open; the logical unit consists of more than one stanza. When the strong-stimulus reaches its end, it resolves considerable logical tensions and constitutes comprehensive units which are more strongly accentuated than light-stimulus and mobile units, i.e. their closure receives a greater amount of emphasis. The reader's expectation does not subside before this closure, as can be judged from the following example by Tennyson:

> Sweet after showers, ambrosial air,
>   That rollest from the gorgeous gloom
>   Of evening over brake and bloom
> And meadow, slowly breathing bare
>
> The round of space, and rapt below
>   Through all the dewy-tasselled wood,
>   And shadowing down the hornèd flood
> In ripples, fan my brows and blow
>
> The feaver from my cheek, and sigh
>   The full new life that feeds thy breath
>   Throughout my frame, till Doubt and Death,
> Ill brethren, let the fancy fly
>
> From belt to belt of crimson seas
>   On leagues of odour streaming far,
>   To where in yonder orient star
> A hundred spirits whisper 'Peace'.
>
> (Tennyson, *In Memoriam*, section 86)

This poem has run-on stanzas throughout. The second stanza connects with the first by way of a noun phrase dependent on the participle 'breathing'; the third stanza also introduces a direct object that is linked to the preceding line; it refers to 'Sweet after showers, ambrosial air' (l. 1); the last stanza completes the subordinate clause that emerges from l. 11. The logical skeleton of this poem can be described as follows: ambrosial air, fan my brows and fill me with new life, until my mind finds peace. The tension that builds up throughout sixteen lines is finally resolved by the word 'Peace'. The individual stanzas seem to lose their identity and merge into one large unit of the whole poem, whose closure is

extremely impressive. *In Memoriam* exhibits so many examples of this kind of structure that several of its sections
resemble stanzaic poems or sonnets whose component units
are hardly accentuated. Sections like nos 86 or 14 show that
the 'sustained movement' attributed to the poem does not depend on its stanza form but on the logical structure of strong-
stimulus stanzas.

We shall try to survey at least the most widespread modes
of *a priori* linkage. Although they are rarely as long as the
ones quoted above, strong-stimuli occur in all periods of
poetry. However, poets before 1800 seem to have been re-
luctant to employ them extensively. Since later poets tend to
disregard the concept of stanzaic unity, strong-stimulus tech-
niques prevail in Romantic, Victorian and modern poetry.

The simplest type of *a priori* progression occurs in stanzas
containing demonstrative pronouns. If they point ahead they
fix the following stanza(s) *a priori*. As in stanzaic
comparison, their syntactic unity is usually retained. A very
similar effect is reached by references to subsequent direct
speech. Blake has combined these two devices in ll. 7–8 of
'The Clod and the Pebble', which I quote in full because it
also contains the light-stimulus version of the same feature.

'Love seeketh not itself to please,
Nor of itself hath any care,
But for another gives its ease,
And builds a Heaven in Hell's despair.'

So sung a little Clod of Clay,
Trodden with the cattle's feet,
But a Pebble of the brook
Warbled out these metres meet:

'Love seeketh only Self to please,
To bind another to its delight,
Joys in another's loss of ease,
And builds a Hell in Heaven's despite.'

Stanzaic linkage *a priori* also results if subordinate clauses precede their main clauses stanzaically. If the first element involves subordination, it causes grammatical tensions which have to be resolved. We may encounter causal and concessive relations, infinitive constructions and that-clauses which precede their main sentence. Temporal and conditional relations of this sort occur most frequently. The following quotation from Shelley's *The Sensitive Plant* shows the structural difference between light- and strong-stimulus once more:

> Whether the Sensitive Plant, or that
> Which within its boughs like a Spirit sat,
> Ere its outward form had known decay,
> Now felt this change, I cannot say.
>
> Whether that Lady's gentle mind,
> No longer with the form combined
> Which scattered love, as stars do light,
> Found sadness, where it left delight,
>
> I dare not guess; ...
>> (Shelley, *The Sensitive Plant*, 'Conclusion', ll. 1–9)

The first stanza is completely self-sufficient and neatly closed by a main clause. The second stanza, which is connected to the initial stanza by a light-stimulus (comparison sensitive plant/lady), is syntactically open. We expect the conclusion of the sentence in the next stanza. Although this second syntactic unit comprises only five lines as compared to four in the first, it creates a completely different expectation in the reader, because it extends beyond the stanzaic boundaries. Since stanza 3 introduces another strong-stimulus ending in l. 16, the stanzas operate merely as formal props and outward demarcations. They contribute little to the intrinsic structure of this part of the poem.

While this is true for most strong-stimulus structures, we may be surprised at the following poem by Blake:

Whether on Ida's shady brow,
Or in the chambers of the East,
The chambers of the sun, that now
From ancient melodies have ceased;

Whether in Heaven ye wander fair,
Or the green corners of the earth,
Or the blue regions of the air
Where the melodious winds have birth;

Whether on crystal rocks ye rove,
Beneath the bosom of the Sea
Wand'ring in many a coral grove,
Fair Nine, forsaking Poetry!

How have you left the ancient love
That bard of old enjoyed in you!
The languid strings do scarcely move,
The sound is forced, the notes are few.
(Blake, 'To the Muses')

The strong-stimulus is as extensive as that in section 86 of *In Memoriam*. However, Blake stresses both the stanzaic and the poetic whole; despite the verb in l. 5, we have two exchangeable stanzas with a subsequent analogous stanza whose position is fixed, because it refers explicitly to the Muses and prepares for the last stanza. These three stanzas are all subordinate to the climax of the poem, which contains the main clause: the speaker's complaint about the decay of poetry. The primary unit is one syntactic whole, yet its parts are sufficiently emphasized to constitute more than merely formal units. The poem's structure seems to resemble that of Shelley's 'Conclusion'; but Blake's composition is more rigorously stanzaic than Shelley's, because its strong-stimulus is set up differently. The overall structure of the poems is quite different. The earlier poem shows that the principles of stanzaic mobility and retrospective linkage can be embedded in, and subordinated to, *a priori* progression; the strong-stimulus constitutes the primary unit.

We have seen that subsequent subordination is perceived as linkage *ex posteriori*: if the stanzaic boundaries separate a main clause from its dependent clause, the stanzas are usually connected by a light-stimulus. Although the main clause is also followed by its dependent clause in defining relative and participle constructions, and in subordinations of purpose that contain the syntactic marker ('So'), stanzaic progression involves a strong-stimulus because the subsequent dependent unit derives its logical roots from the main clause. Furthermore, the dependency is already visible in the main clause, which sets up the expectation of continuance in the reader.

The most radical method of *a priori* progression occurs in stanzas that separate the parts of a sentence. The individual stanzas demarcate no logical subdivisions as in the types mentioned above. Basic logical units are dissociated by stanzaic boundaries. The integrity of logical units conflicts sharply with stanzaic integrity if stanzaic boundaries separate noun phrases from their verb phrases, verb phrases from (object) noun phrases, verbs from their prepositional adjunct, prepositions from their noun phrases, and conjunctions from their clauses. A host of examples could be adduced from poems by Wyatt, Jonson, Herrick, Marvell, Byron, Shelley, Tennyson, Frost, Dylan Thomas, Richard Wilbur and Ted Hughes. I confine myself to a poem by Marianne Moore, who is well known for her idiosyncratic stanza forms:

> wade
> through black jade.
> > Of the crow-blue mussel shells, one keeps
> > adjusting the ash heaps;
> > > opening and shutting itself like

an
injured fan.
   The barnacles which encrust the side
   of the wave, cannot hide
      there for the submerged shafts of the

sun,
split like spun
   glass, move themselves with spotlight swiftness
   into the crevices –
      in and out, illuminating

the
turquoise sea
   of bodies. The water drives a wedge
   of iron through the iron edge
      of the cliff; whereupon the stars,

pink
rice-grains, ink-
   bespattered jellyfish, crabs like green
   lilies, and submarine
      toadstools, slide each on the other.

ac-
cident – lack
   of cornice, dynamite grooves, burns, and
   hatchet strokes, these things stand
      out on it; the chasm side is

dead.
Repeated
   evidence has proved that it can live
   on what can not revive
      its youth. The sea grows old in it.
          (Moore, 'The Fish')

5
Conclusion

It has been our aim to demonstrate that stanzaic composition inevitably poses problems of meaning. Prosodists describe the skeleton of an identically recurring formal element within the poem. Critical analysis, on the other hand, all too often defines poetic structure without considering the stanza as an aspect of meaning. Consequently, most explicators prefer to neglect the stanza. This is not to discredit either prosody or structural poetics. We need the prosodic terminology in order to talk about forms; and poetic structure can be gauged in non-stanzaic terms. But prosody has isolated forms from meaning, and structural poetics has been preoccupied with meaning beyond extrinsic form. We have tried to bridge this gap by suggesting criteria for relating the stanza to poetic structure. We have discussed various strategies through which poets arrive at stanzaic units of meaning. We have also developed a stanzaic concept of poetic structure by evaluating the logical relations among stanzas and their place and function as parts within the poetic whole.

Select bibliography

Texts

Most of the poems mentioned and quoted are contained in the following period anthologies. Their spelling has been followed throughout.

Elizabethan Lyrics, ed. Norman Ault, New York, 1949; 3rd ed., 1970.

The Metaphysical Poets, ed. Helen Gardner, Harmondsworth, 1957; 2nd revised ed., 1966.

Ben Jonson and the Cavalier Poets, ed. Hugh Maclean, New York, 1974.

English Verse, ed. W. Peacock, Vol. III, *From Dryden to Wordsworth*, London, 1963.

English Poetry and Prose of the Romantic Movement, ed. George B. Woods, Chicago, 1950.

Poetry of the Victorian Period, ed. George B. Woods and Jerome H. Buckley, Chicago, 1955.

The Penguin Book of Contemporary Verse 1918–1960, ed. Kenneth Allott, Harmondsworth, revised and enlarged ed., 1962.

The New Poetry, ed. A. Alvarez, Harmondsworth, revised ed., 1966.

The Norton Anthology of Modern Poetry, ed. Richard Ellmann and Robert O'Clair, New York, 1973.

Poems not included in these anthologies can be traced in the *Oxford Standard Authors* (Byron, Carew, Donne, Keats, Shelley, Spenser) and in the following editions. The spelling of Wyatt's poetry has been slightly modernized.

Auden, W. H., *Collected Shorter Poems 1927–1957*, London, 1966.

Campion, Thomas, *Works*, ed. W. R. Davies, New York, 1967.

Herbert, George, *Poems*, ed. H. Gardner, London, 1960.

Sidney, Sir Philip, *Poems*, ed. W. A. Ringler, Jr, Oxford, 1962.

Tennyson, Alfred, Lord, *Poems*, ed. C. Ricks, London, 1969.

Wyatt, Sir Thomas, *Collected Poems*, ed. K. Muir, London, 1967.

Besides the sources quoted in full, the following editions and collections of critical essays and interviews have been consulted for Chapter 1:

Elizabethan Critical Essays, ed. G. G. Smith, 2 vols, Oxford, 1904.

Ben Jonson, *Works*, ed. C. H. Herford and Percy Simpson, Vol. I,

Conversations with Drummond of Hawthorndon (1618–19), Oxford, 1925.

Bysshe, Edward, *The Art of English Poetry* (1702), Scolar Press Facsimile, Menston, 1968.

Hegel, G. W. F., *Ästhetik*, ed. F. Bassenge, 2 vols, Frankfurt, 1955.

Poe, Edgar A., *The Complete Works*, ed. J. A. Harrison, 14 vols, New York, 2nd ed., 1965.

English Critical Texts, ed. D. J. Enright and E. de Chickera, Oxford, 4th ed., 1966.

American Poetic Theory, ed. George Perkins, New York, 1972.

The Poetics of the New American Poetry, ed. D. M. Allen and W. Tallman, New York, 1973.

Prosodical, historical and critical studies

Allen, Gay W., *American Prosody*, New York, 1935.
A good historical and unusually perceptive introduction ranging from Freneau to Dickinson.

Alonso, Damaso, 'Versos plurimembros y poemas correlativos', *Revista de la biblioteca archivo y museo del ayuntamiento de Madrid*, III (1944), pp. 89–191.

Alonso, Damaso, 'Poesia correlativa inglesa en los siglos XVI y XVII', *Filologia Moderna*, II (1961), pp. 1–47.
The first systematic attempts to deal with summative structures; develops basic types of this unduly neglected phenomenon.

Chatman, Seymour, *A Theory of Meter*, The Hague, 1965.
The best introduction to linguistic prosody; based on structural linguistics, it discusses aspects of stress analysis and phonological phenomena.

Fraser, G. S., *Metre, Rhyme and Free Verse*, The Critical Idiom 8, London, 1970.
A valuable introduction, particularly helpful concerning the metre of English verse.

Fucilla, Joseph G., 'A Rhetorical Pattern in Renaissance and Baroque Poetry', *Studies in the Renaissance*, III (1956), pp. 23–48.
Develops Damaso Alonso's approach to correlative verse; an important contribution.

Fussell, Paul, Jr, *Poetic Meter and Poetic Form*, New York, 1965.
A good, if somewhat conventional introduction to problems of metre and poetic structure. Fails to advance problems of meaning in his discussion of form.

Gross, Harvey, *Sound and Form in Modern Poetry. A Study of Prosody from Thomas Hardy to Robert Lowell*, Ann Arbor, 1964.

A reliable and thorough study, which covers all the important aspects of modern verse. Attempts to relate meaning to form, but does not go beyond traditional discussions of the stanza. Attacks some modern prosodical theories, notably the linguists'.

Hamer, Enid, *The Metres of English Poetry*, London, 1930.

The first popular study to present Saintsbury's and Schipper's findings in a condensed form. Largely descriptive, with a good range of examples; too impressionistic at times.

Häublein, Ernst, *Strophe und Struktur in der Lyrik Sir Philip Sidneys*, Frankfurt, 1971.

The first full study of the structural implications of the stanza. Investigates the logical relations among stanzas and their relevance for the poetic whole. Deals with Sidney and Elizabethan *Miscellanies*; extends Alonso's approach by developing the stanzaic aspects of correlative verse. Assesses Sidney's stanzaic technique in his adaptations of the Psalms.

Hayes, Albert M., 'Counterpoint in Herbert', *Studies in Philology*, XXXV (1938), pp. 43–60.

Attempts to classify Herbert's stanza forms by attending to line length; includes tables illustrating stanza forms of sixteenth- and seventeenth-century authors.

Ing, Catherine, *Elizabethan Lyrics. A Study of the Development of English Metres and their Relation to Poetic Effect*, London, 3rd ed., 1971.

Still one of the basic studies of Renaissance and Metaphysical versification, with very valuable chapters on music and poetry.

Johnson, Paula, *Form and Transformation in Music and Poetry of the English Renaissance*, New Haven, 1972.

Applies the approach of *Gestalt* psychology to aspects of serial art; finds sequential structures in music and poetry and discusses several types of 'segmental' and 'continuous' structures. A valuable, if theoretically deficient, study with somewhat sweeping historical conclusions.

Malof, Joseph, *A Manual of English Meters*, Bloomington, 1970.

The most valuable manual for the student who is not preoccupied with the stanza. Provides a full treatment of all metrical terms; with Stewart the best discussion of folk metres; summarizes all the aspects of stress and rhythm; acceptable for all metrical schools including linguists; excellent glossary.

Olson, Elder, '"Sailing to Byzantium": Prolegomena to a Poetics of the Lyric', *University of Kansas City Review*, VII (1942), pp. 209–19.

A very interesting application of the neo-Aristotelian concept of *dynamis* to lyric poetry, which may serve as a point of departure for a structural approach.

Pattison, Bruce, *Music and Poetry of the English Renaissance*, London, 2nd ed., 1970.

One of the most delightful and perceptive studies, with many insights into problems of form and stanza.

Prasuhn, Klaus-Ulrich, *Zur Erfüllung der Spenserstanze bei Edmund Spenser, Lord Byron und John Keats*, Diss. Göttingen, 1974.

A good historical summary, which fails to tackle problems of poetic structure.

Preminger, Alex, Warnke, Frank J., and Hardison, O. B., Jr, *Princeton Encyclopedia of Poetry and Poetics*, Princeton, 2nd and enlarged ed., 1974.

A brilliant handbook.

Riesz, János, *Die Sestine. Ihre Stellung in her literarishen Kritik und ihre Geschichte als lyrisches Genus*, Munich, 1971.

The most extensive comparatistic treatment of the sestina so far. Discusses a great number of examples and traces its history from the troubadours to contemporary poets.

Saintsbury, George, *A History of English Prosody*, 3 vols, New York, 1906–10; 2nd ed., 1923.

With Schipper the classic descriptive manual for stanza forms.

Schipper, Josef, *Neuenglische Metrik*, 3 vols, Bonn, 1881–8.

The third volume contains the classification of stanza forms. Exhaustive, if over-systematic discussion; the most complete treatment, but difficult to use.

Schlawe, Fritz, *Die deutschen Strophenformen*, Stuttgart, 1972.

A complete list of stanza forms found in the poetry of sixty German poets from 1600 to 1950; systematic-chronological statistics developed with the help of computers, which should lead the way to similar ventures for English poetry.

Schliebs, Gisela, *Die Funktion der Strophenformen in George Herbert's 'The Temple' im Rahmen des literarhistorischen sowie des musik- und dichtungstheoretischen Kontextes*, Diss. Giessen, 1970.

Links Herbert to the formal tradition of the sixteenth century and discusses his stanzaic technique; stresses hymnal aspects of Herbert's poetry, discusses his poetic theory and provides thorough analyses. An unnecessarily hefty study, which does not deal with logical relations or stanzaic unity.

Shapiro, Karl, and Beum, Robert, *A Prosody Handbook*, New York, 1965.
With Malof the most valuable introduction to prosody, with excellent comments on the stanza.

Smith, Barbara Herrstein, *Poetic Closure. A Study how Poems End*, Chicago, 1968.
A fundamental and brilliant book on poetic structure; the best available study on closural aspects of poems.

Stewart, G. R., Jr, 'The Meter of the Popular Ballad', *PMLA*, XL (1925), pp. 933–62.

Stewart, G. R., Jr, *The Technique of English Verse*, New York, 1930; 2nd ed., 1958.
These two studies provide the most important discussions of ballad metre in developing the concept of dipodic structure.

Thompson, John, *The Founding of English Metre*, London, 1961.
A superb study of Elizabethan verse, which concentrates on the iambic pentameter; the definitive treatment of Elizabethan prosody, excluding stanzaic aspects.

Tierney, Frank M., 'The Development of the Rondeau in England from its Origin in the Middle Ages to its Revival in the Years Following 1860', *Revue de l'Université d'Ottawa*, XLI (1971), pp. 25–46.

Tierney, Frank M., 'The Causes of the Revival of the Rondeau in 19th Century England', *Revue de l'Université d'Ottawa*, XLIII (1973), pp. 96–113.
Traces the development of the rondeau in England; unfortunately, he does not analyse the poems mentioned.

Weiss, Wolfgang, *Der Refrain in der elisabethanischen Lyrik*, Diss. Munich, 1964.
A very illuminating study, whose findings should be applied to other periods.

Weiss, Wolfgang, 'Die Airs im Stilwandel', *Anglia*, LXXXVII (1969), pp. 201–16.
Investigates the structure of air poems; could be extended into a monograph on airs.

Wimsatt, William K. (ed), *Versification. Major Language Types*, New York, 1972.
Sixteen essays dealing with metrical problems of languages; with a good bibliography; stanzaic problems are totally neglected.

Index